Cambridge Opera Handbooks

W. A. Mozart
Die Entführung aus dem Serail

W. A. Mozart
Die Entführung aus dem Serail

THOMAS BAUMAN

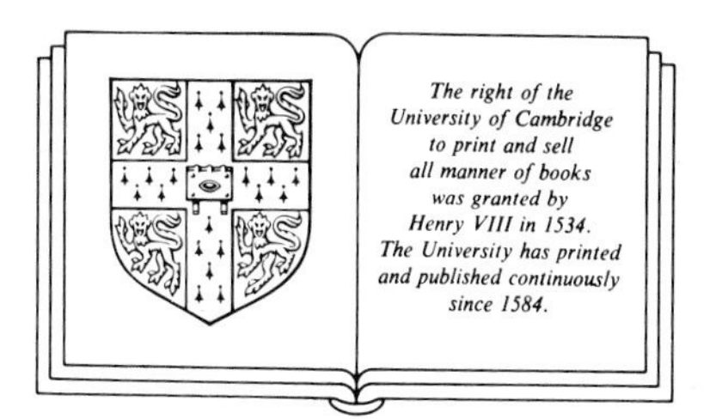

CAMBRIDGE UNIVERSITY PRESS

Cambridge
New York New Rochelle Melbourne Sydney

Published by the Press Syndicate of the University of Cambridge
The Pitt Building, Trumpington Street, Cambridge CB2 1RP
32 East 57th Street, New York, NY 10022, USA
10 Stamford Road, Oakleigh, Melbourne 3166, Australia

First published 1987

Printed in Great Britain at
the University Press, Cambridge

British Library cataloguing in publication data

Bauman, Thomas
W. A. Mozart, Die Entführung aus dem
Serail. - (Cambridge opera handbooks).
1. Mozart, Wolfgang Amadeus
Entführung aus dem Serail, Die
I. Title
782.1'092'4 ML410.M9

Library of Congress cataloguing in publication data

Bauman, Thomas, 1948–
W. A. Mozart, Die Entführung aus dem Serail.
(Cambridge opera handbooks)
Bibliography.
Discography.
Includes index.
1. Mozart, Wolfgang Amadeus, 1756–1791. Entführung
aus dem Serail. I. Title. II. Title: Entführung aus
dem Serail. III. Series.
ML410.M9B185 1987 782.1'092'4 87-10326

ISBN 0 521 32545 5 hard covers
ISBN 0 521 31060 1 paperback

ME

For Emily and Rebecca

Contents

Illustrations

CAMBRIDGE OPERA HANDBOOKS

General preface

This is a series of studies of individual operas written for the opera-goer or record-collector as well as the student or scholar. Each volume has three main concerns: historical, analytical and interpretative. There is a detailed description of the genesis of each work, the collaboration between librettist and composer, and the first performance and subsequent stage history. A full synopsis considers the opera as a structure of musical and dramatic effects, and there is also a musical analysis of a section of the score. The analysis, like the history, shades naturally into interpretation: by a careful combination of new essays and excerpts from classic statements the editors of the handbooks show how critical writing about the opera, like the production and performance, can direct or distort appreciation of its structural elements. A final section of documents gives a select bibliography, a discography, and guides to other sources. Each book is published in both hard covers and as a paperback.

Books published
Richard Wagner: *Parsifal* by Lucy Beckett
W. A. Mozart: *Don Giovanni* by Julian Rushton
C. W. von Gluck: *Orfeo* by Patricia Howard
Igor Stravinsky: *The Rake's Progress* by Paul Griffiths
Leoš Janáček: *Kát'a Kabanová* by John Tyrrell
Giuseppe Verdi: *Falstaff* by James A. Hepokoski
Benjamin Britten: *Peter Grimes* by Philip Brett
Giacomo Puccini: *Tosca* by Mosco Carner
Benjamin Britten: *The Turn of the Screw* by Patricia Howard
Richard Strauss: *Der Rosenkavalier* by Alan Jefferson
Claudio Monteverdi: *Orfeo* by John Whenham
Giacomo Puccini: *La bohème* by Arthur Groos and Roger Parker
Giuseppe Verdi: *Otello* by James A. Hepokoski
Benjamin Britten: *Death in Venice* by Donald Mitchell
W. A. Mozart: *Le nozze di Figaro* by Tim Carter

Acknowledgments

I owe a pleasant debt of collegial gratitude to Daniel Heartz and Karol Berger. What follows has benefited considerably from their careful reading and suggestions. Research in Austria for this volume was made possible by a generous Pew Foundation Grant from Stanford University.

The illustrations in this book appear by kind permission of the following: Plate 1, The Library of Congress; Plate 2, Bild-Archiv der österreichischen Nationalbibliothek; Plate 3; Historisches Museum der Stadt Wien; Plate 4, Bild-Archiv der österreichischen Nationalbibliothek; Plate 5*a*, Metropolitan Opera Archives; Plate 5*b*, Glyndebourne Festival Opera 1968; Plate 6*a* and *b*, Pressebüro Salzburger Festspiele; Plate 7*a* and *b*, Teatro alla Scala, Archivio Fotografico; Plate 8, The Library of Congress.

1 *Introduction*

'Now the day before yesterday Stephanie the Younger gave me a libretto to set', wrote Mozart to his father on 1 August 1781. 'The book is quite good. The subject is Turkish, and it's called *Bellmont* und *konstanze.* or *die verführung aus dem Serail.*'[1] With this amusing slip ('seduction' for 'abduction') Mozart announced his preliminary work on a libretto which grew over the next ten months into *Die Entführung aus dem Serail.* Suffused with youthful confidence in its creator's maturing dramatic powers, this opera more than any other work carried Mozart's name over the next decade to every corner of the German-speaking world.

Especially in the non-German-speaking world, however, the position of *Die Entführung aus dem Serail* as an unequivocal masterpiece has been far more tenuous than that of Mozart's later comic operas. The dramatic weight borne by the spoken dialogue, so much greater here than in *Die Zauberflöte*, has played a significant role in critical misgivings; the story itself has been judged – particularly by later standards – as far too insubstantial and naive, even for an opera. Some have gone so far as to relegate Mozart's music itself to a lower dramatic plane. Most notably, Edward Dent set up a chorus of disappointment among modern writers who lament the opera's lack of stylistic unity – an opinion one can find among the work's earliest critics as well.[2]

The two problems of dialogue and style are part of the same aesthetic issue, for the role played by the spoken word in an opera like the *Entführung* directly affects the musician's ability to shape and articulate the drama. Certainly, by the standards of Mozart's own day, only a perverse listener would have regarded the dialogue of a German opera as so much pedestrian manoeuvring in preparation for sublime moments of music-dramatic expression. In Vienna as in other centres, German operas not only shared many features with spoken dramas, but also alternated with them on the same stage and often shared many of the same singer–players. A historical appreciation of *Die Entführung aus dem Serail* requires us to acknowledge its proximity to the German tradition of spoken plays with musical enhancement.

It also allows us to see more clearly what sets it apart from virtually everything in the German repertory that had preceded it – Mozart's own unwillingness to accept these limitations. The notion of musical enhancement had to yield to transfiguration at moments where operatic demands supersede those of the spoken drama – the quartet closing Act II, for instance, or the lovers' recitative and duet near the end of Act III.

No one had ever written anything like this music before in a German comic opera. Is the *Entführung* as a result fundamentally different from all the lowly specimens of this genre which preceded it, and about which we know so little? Carl Maria von Weber thought so. Despite its mixing of 'the most consummate conception of dramatic truth and characteristic declamation' with 'an incomplete renunciation here and there of the conventional in form and shape', he saw in the *Entführung* not only a unique repository of Mozart's youthful vigour but also the watershed in the composer's artistic coming of age and the basis for everything that followed in his later operatic masterpieces:

> I venture to express the belief that in the *Entführung* Mozart's artistic experience had reached its maturity, and thereafter only life experience created on. The world was justified in expecting more operas like *Figaro* and *Don Juan* from him; but with the best will he could not write another *Entführung*.[3]

The circumstances in which Mozart found German opera in 1781 and under which he composed *Die Entführung aus dem Serail* created an uneasy dialectic between received notions of German comic opera as plays enlivened with interspersed musical numbers and the overpowering, primary role Mozart had come to realise music could play in composing *Idomeneo* for Munich in 1780. The mixed dramatic character of the *Entführung* offered an additional basis for creative unease in the young composer. Just before he began work on the *Entführung*, Mozart had remarked in a letter to his father on 16 June 1781 that he regarded comic and serious opera as divergent styles – and further, that the Viennese view agreed with his own sense of their incompatibility:

> Do you think, then, that I would compose an Opera Comique in the same way as an Opera Seria? – However little playfulness there should be in an

Opera Seria and however much of the learned and reasonable, just so little of the learned must there be in an Opera Buffa and so much more of the playful and comic. I can't help it if in an Opera Seria people wish to have comic music as well; – here, however, one distinguishes very clearly in this matter.

But by the time Mozart completed the *Entführung* the distinction was by no means so clear. As with everything Mozart wrote for the stage, the final shape of the opera sprang as much from external circumstances as from internal impulse. To set forth these circumstances and their significance for the opera as we know it today is no simple task. We begin here with how and why *Belmont und Constanze* – a libretto written for a conservative northern composer and already produced in 1781 at Berlin – should have been put in Mozart's hands for a new Viennese production later that year.

Vienna and the National Singspiel

When Mozart arrived in Vienna on 16 March 1781 the local court-supported company which performed German opera, the National Singspiel, had just concluded its third season. Joseph II had seen to the creation of this enterprise in 1778 as a musical adjunct to the city's National Theatre, which he had instituted two years earlier.

The National Theatre and National Singspiel performed together at the 'Theater nächst der kaiserlichen Burg' or 'Burgtheater'. This stage and the nearby Kärntnerthor Theatre were both owned by the imperial court. The Burgtheater was the smaller of the two buildings, but more prestigious: in Viennese minds it was closely associated with the emperor, both physically and as an extension of imperial patronage and policy. The association became even stronger with the creation of the National Theatre and Singspiel.

The local cultural observer Johann Pezzl defined a 'national stage' as 'one which performs in the language of its nation, and whose pieces depict as much as possible the nation's customs, and tailor themselves to the genius and interest of the people attending them'.[4] The National Theatre at least approximated to Pezzl's ideal, but the National Singspiel inevitably fell far short of it, for Viennese musical taste in opera was anything but 'national'.

Such a state of affairs was by no means surprising. Despite the efforts of Philip Hafner, Joseph Felix Kurz-Bernardon and Franz Josef Haydn during the 1750s and 1760s, German-language opera in Austria continued to favour the improvised farce with music, featuring local variants of the *commedia dell'arte* masks. Such entertainments were not to be tolerated on an enlightened emperor's stage, which ought to be a school for morals and decency, and so they left the imperial stages (where they had been welcome under Emperor Francis Stephan) and migrated to the suburban theatres that began springing to life after Joseph II's Theaterfreiheit Edict of 1776. German opera of a more 'regular' sort was already leading a healthy existence at that date, but remained overwhelmingly a central and north German product. The Viennese admired these works as dramas, but the music left them cold ('too Lutheran' said Mozart's first Belmonte of their vocal style).

The Viennese dramatist Tobias von Gebler explained quite candidly what the emperor demanded in a letter written in early 1778 to the Berlin *lumière* Friedrich Nicolai:

> You honourable people will perhaps have heard that our truly *German* emperor is now founding a German opera, for the serious as well as comic genre. Yet we must have nothing but true musical virtuosos and no street-singers, and the music, too, must be of the sort that we are used to here by Piccinni, Anfossi, Paisiello, and to an extent Grétry.[5]

During its first years the National Singspiel did assemble a cadre of excellent singers as the emperor had wished, as well as a splendid orchestra and chorus. The repertory to be performed by these musicians proved more problematical. Commissions went out to local composers and poets for new works, but production could not keep up with demand in either quantity or quality. Recourse was had almost at once to successful opéras-comiques of Monsigny, Gossec, Dezède, and above all Grétry; soon thereafter the theatre turned to opera buffa as well (Pietro Guglielmi, Gassmann, Sacchini and Anfossi). In other words, the situation reverted to the way things had been before 1778.

In contrast, the National Singspiel took up very few works originating from other German stages. The enterprise's primary commitment, in theory and in practice alike, lay with local composers. For them the National Singspiel and its superb resources represented an unprecedented opportunity, but prior to Mozart's arrival, only one Austrian had profited from it – Ignaz Umlauf. He was serving as principal violist in the small orchestra which played for the National Theatre, when in late 1777 the court commissioned him to set the one-act opera *Die Bergknappen* for a small operatic wing the emperor was hoping to create at the Burgtheater. On the strength of its success Joseph II decided in early 1778 to make the

National Singspiel a permanent institution. Umlauf was appointed its Kapellmeister. He composed two further operas for the enterprise's first two seasons and was completing a fourth when Mozart came to Vienna in March 1781.

At their best, the German operas Umlauf wrote for the National Singspiel not only reveal a popular tunefulness, they also supply details of ambiance, characterisation and orchestral colour seldom encountered in scores from the North. The first aria of *Das Irrlicht* (1782), for example, acquaints us at once with the arch-innocent heroine Blanka and her simple country surroundings by means of a bucolic, transparent *alla siciliana* melody supported by an opening drone and delightful anticipations in the bass (Ex. 1*a*). Umlauf does not forget for whom he is writing, either – Aloysia Lange, the most celebrated of the early interpreters of the part of Constanze in the *Entführung*. Toward the end he sends her rocketing up to an astonishing high a‴ that would dizzy even Blanka's nightingale friend in the aria text, which presumably inspired this flight (Ex. 1*b*). Umlauf saves the solo oboe for this one passage, and also keeps a solo clarinet silent until it offers its benediction in the closing ritornello.

Gebler described Umlauf's operas as 'solid and pleasing', and they proved to be to the taste of Vienna at large in their congenial blending of tunefulness, buffo style, local folk elements and virtuosic display. From the beginning Mozart was keenly aware of Umlauf as a

Ex. 1*a*

Ex. 1*b*

rival, which may in part account for the uniformly disparaging remarks he made about Umlauf's music in his letters to his father.

Stephanie and Vienna's window to the north

The two operas Umlauf composed around the time of Mozart's appearance at Vienna – *Die schöne Schusterin* and *Das Irrlicht* – were adapted for the National Singspiel by the man who collaborated with Mozart on the revision of *Belmont und Constanze*, Gottlieb Stephanie the Younger. During the Seven Years' War he had come to Austria as a Prussian prisoner of war. He carved out an influential position for himself in Viennese theatrical life as an actor, dramatist, and later director. He was appointed as one of the five inspectors of the National Theatre in 1776, and at the end of Carneval 1781 the direction of the National Singspiel was put in his hands. This in effect made him directly responsible to the emperor's personal overseer of theatrical affairs, the 'General-Spektakel-Direktor' Count Franz Xaver Rosenberg-Orsini.

Stephanie was not only one of the most powerful men in Viennese theatrical circles, he was also one of the most hated and vilified. Mozart's brother-in-law, the actor Joseph Lange, recalled that Stephanie 'tyrannised over everything, and as a result was universally hated'.[6] Mozart himself learnt of Stephanie's ill fame after only a few months in Vienna. On 16 June 1781 he wrote to Leopold concerning Stephanie:

> This man has the worst reputation throughout Vienna – for which I am very sorry – as a rude, deceitful, slanderous man, who inflicts the greatest injustices on people. But I'm not getting mixed up in any of that. It may be true, since everyone carps about it. Nevertheless, he carries the greatest weight with the emperor, and he was very friendly toward me from the first, and said 'We're already old friends [he had first met Mozart in 1773] and I am glad if I can be in a position to help you.'

Mozart stressed something else about Stephanie in this letter: he was a man who understood the theatre, a virtue Mozart held in the highest esteem. By 1781 Stephanie's theatrical competence extended to German opera as well. More than anyone else, Stephanie had been the National Singspiel's literary work-horse, serving from its inception as its principal translator and adapter. By the time of the première of *Die Entführung aus dem Serail* he had translated nine French operas and four Italian ones (for use with the original music) and had adapted three other texts for new settings by local composers.

In the National Theatre's repertory many of the most successful original German dramas came from outside Austria despite the activities of many local dramatists, Stephanie among them. It was only natural, under these circumstances, for the National Singspiel to look northward as well for readily accessible German librettos that could serve as vehicles for local composers. Viennese adapters of these northern texts were not indiscriminate, however. The earliest phase of the German libretto's cultivation in the north found little resonance at Vienna. Theatrical taste was, like fashion, a mercurial and fickle thing there. One seized the moment and strove studiously to remain *au courant*, as many of Mozart's own remarks in his letters tell us.

In all of Germany, the most popular librettist around 1780 was the Leipzig businessman Christoph Friedrich Bretzner. In 1779 he had published a set of four comic opera texts, each a departure from earlier paths and each set many times by composers all across Germany during the next few years. As far as the musical structure of these texts is concerned, they offered nothing new to German opera.

Characterisation, the conduct of the plot and scenic construction are almost entirely the creation of the dialogue, making these works little different from spoken comedies and farces. The musical items consist mostly of solo songs, strewn about here and there with little regard for how they fit into a scene. Many are short and aphoristic, and often a single character will be given three, four or even five numbers in a row to sing. Dramatic ensembles and finales are nowhere to be found. All of this reflected accurately Bretzner's northern legacy.

Yet such conservative features did not deter German composers from embracing Bretzner's librettos for their cleverness, charm, and above all their colourful and novel plots. No one in the north had thought of bringing Molière to German operatic stages before (as in *Adrast und Isidore*), or of exploiting the grisly and supernatural side of medieval German legends (*Das wütende Heer*), or of turning the spirit of Gozzi's fables to operatic account (*Der Irrwisch*).

Vienna was intrigued as well. All four of Bretzner's librettos were adapted there for local composers during the 1780s. The most important of these adaptations was the revision of *Der Irrwisch* which Stephanie undertook for Umlauf in late 1780, retitled *Das Irrlicht*. We shall have occasion to mention this project several times later on, for it ran a course remarkably parallel to that run by *Belmont und Constanze* on its way to becoming *Die Entführung aus dem Serail*.

Mozart and the search for a German libretto

In 1781 Bretzner published his fifth libretto, a markedly different work from his earlier efforts – *Belmont und Constanze, oder Die Entführung aus dem Serail*. He had written it in 1780 for Johann André, the popular Kapellmeister of the Döbbelin company, resident at Berlin. The opera capitalised on the burgeoning vogue of Turkish operas (a subject we shall deal with in Chapter 3), and also presented several important technical advances in the musical construction of a German libretto. But no doubt the name of its author was the decisive factor in Stephanie's mind when he presented it to Mozart on 30 July 1781 after months of casting about for a text suitable for the young composer and for the National Singspiel.

That March Mozart had already shown Stephanie another Turkish opera he had brought with him to Vienna, the one we now know as *Zaïde*. We do not have the dialogue for Mozart's opera, but one thing is clear from the music: it was unusually serious in tone and high-minded in sentiment for a German opera (some elements appear to be derived from Voltaire's verse tragedy *Zaïre*). The opera's serious complexion sealed its fate as far as the National Singspiel was concerned: Stephanie rejected the work at once, but offered to give Mozart a new piece,

> and, as he says, a good one. . .I could not really disagree with Stephanie. I only said that the work (except for the long dialogues – which are nevertheless easy to change) is very good, but isn't for Vienna, where one prefers to see comic pieces (18 April 1781).

Mozart's remark about Viennese taste invites us to look for a moment at what the National Singspiel was in fact up to at that time. Table 1 summarises the most popular offerings during the 1780/81 season and the first half of the next one, with items ranked by number of performances during that time. A total of thirty different works were put on, twelve of them French, nine Austrian, six Italian and three German. French operas (eight of them by Grétry) dominated during the season preceding Mozart's arrival, but diminished significantly during 1781 in favour of Italian works.

The most successful of the operas listed in Table 1 share several common traits. The two most popular of all – Gluck's *La Rencontre imprévue* (1763) and Grétry's *Zémire et Azor* (1771) – represent revivals of older works with both exotic settings and a mixture of serious and comic characters. Below them are four operas of frankly comic stamp seasoned with a strong dose of ridicule. In particular, *Der Rauchfangkehrer* (about an Italian chimney-sweep who outwits a group of pretentious German lovers) and *I filosofi immaginari* (mocking the mania for intellectual attainments which possesses a father and daughter) dominated the repertory of the National Singspiel during Mozart's first months at Vienna. They also represent the early stirrings of a popular preference which two years later brought about the demise of the German enterprise and the reinstatement of opera buffa at the Burgtheater.

Mozart spent the rest of April engaged in Viennese concert life, waiting for Stephanie to write him a libretto, and growing increasingly disgusted with his employer, the Archbishop Colloredo. In early May the strain culminated in his rude ejection from His Grace's service. From then on Mozart devoted himself to reassuring his disgruntled father that he had acted honourably, that everyone in Vienna despised Colloredo anyway, that he was working hard and making money there, and that his prospects for recognition and

Table 1 *The most popular operas given by the National Singspiel, March 1780–September 1781*

Title [acts] (Librettist–composer)	1st Nat'l Singspiel performance	performances 3/80–2/81	4/81–9/81	Total
La Rencontre imprévue [3] (Dancourt–Gluck)	26 Jul 1780	11	4	15
Zémire et Azor [4] (Marmontel–Grétry)	13 Oct 1779	10	3	13
I filosofi immaginari [2] (Bertati–Paisiello)	22 May 1781	–	11	11
L'incognita perseguitata [3] (Petrosellini–Anfossi)	21 Aug 1780	7	4	11
Le Tonnelier [1] (Poinsinet–Audinot & Gossec)	29 Jun 1780	9	1	10
Der Rauchfangkehrer [3] (Auenbrugger–Salieri)	30 Apr 1781	–	9	9
Was erhält die Männer treu [2] (Zehnmark–Ruprecht)	30 Mar 1780	7	1	8
Die schöne Schusterinn [2] (Stephanie–Umlauf)	22 Jun 1779	4	3	7
L'Ami de la maison [3] (Marmontel–Grétry)	25 May 1778	3	3	6
La Fausse Magie [1] (Marmontel–Grétry)	27 Oct 1778	4	2	6
L'Amant jaloux [2] (d'Hèle–Grétry)	12 Oct 1780	4	1	5
L'isola d'amore [2] (Gori–Sacchini)	7 May 1780	5	0	5
La Rosière de Salencie [3] (Favart–Philidor, Duni *et al.*)	29 Sep 1779	5	0	5

advancement were bright. By the end of May he had made several important friends among Vienna's nobility, including Count Rosenberg. In early June, before leaving for the summer, the count entrusted the responsibility for finding a suitable libretto for Mozart to Friedrich Ludwig Schröder, one of Germany's greatest actors, engaged that April by the National Theatre.

By mid-June Schröder had hunted up a four-act libretto. He gave it to Stephanie, who found the first act strong but the later ones less satisfactory. He also feared it would not be accepted by Rosenberg.

In consequence, Mozart refused to look at it, much less begin work on it. The unknown libretto[7] was never mentioned again.

Mozart returned to his hopes of a new opera from Stephanie himself. But Stephanie, as we shall learn later on, was a busy man who hoped to satisfy Mozart with a minimum of creative energy expended on his own part. The next news we hear of the project is that at the end of July Stephanie handed Bretzner's *Belmont und Constanze* over to Mozart.

2 *Conception and creation*

When Stephanie hit upon *Belmont und Constanze* as an apt libretto for his friend Mozart, the name of its author alone would have recommended it to him, as we noticed in Chapter 1. But there were also other, more immediate considerations bearing upon his decision. The interplay of artistic and practical issues governing the very choice of the libretto continued to guide the project to completion over the next ten months.

Early work: singers and Russian guests

In July of 1781 the Habsburg court was astir with plans for a state visit to be paid in mid-September by Grand Duke Paul Petrovich of Russia and his wife, Princess Sophia Dorothea of Württemberg. Theatrical festivities always played a part in such state occasions, and Stephanie was quick to see in the Russian visit an opportunity to ingratiate the National Singspiel and his friend Mozart with the court. Umlauf already had a new opera ready to help celebrate the occasion, his recently completed setting of Bretzner's *Das Irrlicht*; now Stephanie could also offer a bonus – a Turkish opera by the same popular author, one which his friend Mozart was prepared to compose in the space of a single month.

It is difficult to imagine at this stage that Stephanie intended to do much, if anything, to Bretzner's *Belmont und Constanze.* By itself the libretto offered several clear advantages, given the pressing circumstances. The plot was extremely simple and contained nothing the censor could possibly object to. Unlike Bretzner's earlier librettos with their clutter of songs, this one contained only fifteen numbers, and just seven of these were arias. The ensembles were all brilliant pieces of confrontation between strongly etched personalities, in line with Italianate practice. And the opera already had its own finale – of sorts – for at its dramatic centre of gravity Bretzner had placed its musical centrepiece as well: a massive action quintet with chorus, encompassing the entire elopement episode. Though a daring innovation in the north, where composers had little if any experience with the finale technique of opera buffa, such an extended musical tableau was nothing new to the Viennese. Indeed, in adapting Bretzner's *Der Irrwisch* for Umlauf as *Das Irrlicht*, Stephanie himself had only recently seen fit to rework the end of Act II into a true finale.

There was every reason to believe, then, that Mozart would be able to compose Bretzner's new libretto quickly and without any extensive changes. Such was not to be the case. In fact, of all Mozart's major operas *Die Entführung aus dem Serail* took the longest to complete. To help us clarify the stages by which it emerged from *Belmont und Constanze* we have set out in Table 2 the musical numbers of Bretzner's original libretto and of the version Mozart finally set, in parallel columns. In the table and in the following discussion the prefix 'B' has been used to distinguish the numbering in Bretzner's version from the one familiar to us from Mozart's score.

After receiving the libretto, Mozart set to work at once with vibrant enthusiasm. In a single day he composed B2, B4 and B5. As was always the case with Mozart, the cast of singers had been chosen before he began composing their arias. Some of the German company's finest voices were assigned to the new opera. Josef Valentin Adamberger, the first Belmonte and the troupe's premier tenor, had sung in Italy with great success from 1762 to 1772 under an Italianised version of his name, Adamonti; later he had earned equal esteem at Munich and London before being called to the National Singspiel in 1780.

Caterina Cavalieri, destined to be Constanze, had by all accounts very little in the way of acting ability, but she possessed one of the most brilliant soprano voices anywhere, an instrument in which Mozart revelled all his life. A native of Vienna, she too had Italianised her name (originally Franziska Kavalier) and had been trained at least in part by Salieri, whose mistress she was reputed to have been. She elicited dazzling virtuosic passages from the Viennese composers who wrote for her from the very beginning of her involvement with the National Singspiel.

The basso profondo Johann Ignaz Ludwig Fischer drew Mozart's special musical attention. When Stephanie and Mozart first set about changing Bretzner's libretto in mid-September, they turned their attention first of all to him and to the role of Osmin: 'Since we intended the role of Osmin for Herr Fischer, who has a really excel-

Table 2 *The musical items in* Belmont und Constanze *and* Die Entführung aus dem Serail

	Bretzner: *Belmont und Constanze* (Leipzig, 1781)		Bretzner/Stephanie: *Die Entführung* (Vienna, 1782)
		ACT I	
		1.	Hier soll ich dich denn sehen (Belmonte)
B1.	Wer ein Liebchen hat gefunden (Osmin)	2.	ditto
			Verwünscht seist du (Belmonte-Osmin)
		3.	Solche hergelaufne Laffen (Osmin)
B2.	O wie ängstlich (Belmonte)	4.	ditto
		5a.	March
B3.	Singt dem grossen Bassa Lieder (Janissary chorus)	5b.	ditto
B4.	Ach, ich liebte (Constanze)	6.	ditto
B5.	Marsch! Marsch! Marsch! (Osmin-Pedrillo-Belmonte)	7.	ditto
		ACT II	
B6.	Durch Zärtlichkeit und Schmeicheln (Blonde)	8.	ditto
		9.	Ich gehe, doch rathe ich dir (Osmin-Blonde)
		10.	[Recit.:] Welcher Wechsel herrscht in meinem Herzen –
B7.	Traurigkeit ward mir zum Loose (Constanze)		[Aria:] ditto
B8.	Rondeau: Hofnung, Trösterin im Leiden! (Blonde-Constanze)		
		11.	Martern aller Arten (Constanze)
		12.	Welche Wonne, welche Lust (Blonde)
B9.	Frisch zum Kampfe! (Pedrillo)	13.	ditto

Table 2 (*cont.*)

Bretzner: *Belmont und Constanze* (Leipzig, 1781)	Bretzner/Stephanie: *Die Entführung* (Vienna, 1782)
B10. Vivat, Bachus! (Pedrillo-Osmin)	14. ditto
	15. Wenn der Freude Thränen fliessen (Belmonte)
dialogue	16. Ach Belmonte! ach mein Leben (Constanze-Belmonte-Pedrillo-Blonde)
B11. Mit Pauken und Trompeten (Pedrillo-Blonde-Constanze-Belmonte)	
ACT III	
B12. Welch ängstliches Beben (Belmonte-Pedrillo-Constanze-Blonde-Osmin-Guards)	17. Ich baue ganz auf Deine Stärke (Belmonte)
	dialogue
[Includes:] In Mohrenland gefangen war (Pedrillo)	18. ditto
	dialogue
	19. O! wie will ich triumphiren (Osmin)
[Transformation]	
	20. [Recit.:] Welch' Geschick, O Qual der Seele – [Duet:] Meinetwegen sollst du sterben (Belmonte-Constanze)
B13. Ach, von deinem Arm umschlungen (Belmonte-Constanze)	
B14. Ah, mit freudigem Entzücken (Constanze)	21a. Nie werd ich deine Huld verkennen (Belmonte-Constanze-Pedrillo-Blonde-Osmin)
B15. Oft wölkt stürmisch sich der Himmel! (Chorus)	21b. Bassa Selim lebe lange (Janissary chorus)

lent bass voice. . .such a man has to be made use of, especially since he has the public here wholly on his side' (26 September 1781). Although Fischer had not been to Italy, he had studied with one of Germany's greatest tenors in the seria tradition, Anton Raaff. After working at Mannheim and Munich he came to Vienna in 1780.

Therese Teyber and Johann Ernst Dauer, who created the comic pair Blonde and Pedrillo, were as highly regarded for their acting abilities as for their singing. They both excelled in portraying astute and charming servants, but they also took leading roles from time to time (in Paisiello's *I filosofi immaginari*, for example). Dauer was actually employed by the National Theatre and appeared frequently in spoken dramas.

The value of all these singers to the National Singspiel is reflected in crass economic terms by their salaries. A sampling of what various individuals received around 1781 appears in Table 3. Perhaps the most striking figure is the high salary paid to Adamberger, compared with Cavalieri and Fischer – an advantage for which he had his training and success in Italy to thank.

Table 3 *Representative salaries of members of the Viennese National Theatre and National Singspiel (in florins)*

Name	Position	Salary
Schröder, Friedrich Ludwig	actor	2,550
Adamberger, Josef Valentin	tenor (Belmonte)	2,133
Lange, Aloysia	soprano	1,706
Weidner, Christiane	actress	1,660
Stephanie, Gottlieb	actor	1,400
Fischer, Johann Ludwig	bass (Osmin)	1,200
Cavalieri, Catarina	soprano (Constanze)	1,200
Dauer, Johann Ernst	tenor–actor (Pedrillo)	1,200
Umlauf, Ignaz	Kapellmeister	850
Jautz, Dominik Josef	actor (Pasha Selim)	800
Teyber, Therese	soprano (Blonde)	800
Oboe, clarinet, bassoon, first horn players		750
Concertmaster		450
Other string players, second horn and flute players		350

Source: F. L. W. Meyer: *Friedrich Ludwig Schröder* (Hamburg, 1823), vol. 1, pp. 355–7

The first two arias Mozart had composed on 1 August were for Adamberger and Cavalieri (B2 and B4 in Table 2); at this time he had also set the trio which closes Act I (B5). A week later he had finished Osmin's G minor Lied (B1) and the first Janissary chorus (B3). Act I as Bretzner had planned it was now completely composed. But in late August Mozart learnt that the visit of the Russian grand duke had been put off until November. Immediately he and Stephanie set about expanding the music's role in the completed act. Mozart got Stephanie to turn Belmonte's opening monologue into 'an arietta' and the dialogue following Osmin's Lied into an action duet.

He had also given some music for a new aria intended for Osmin to Stephanie, who manufactured an appropriate text to put under it (No. 3, 'Solche hergelaufne Laffen'). We may recall that Stephanie was an old hand at this, having put new German texts under the music of many a French and Italian opera he had translated for the National Singspiel. Mozart had also finished the overture by early September. In his later operas he was to reserve the composition of this item for last, but here it could not be separated conceptually from Belmonte's arietta, which is foreshadowed in C minor as the overture's contrasting middle section.

Mozart reported all of these activities to Leopold in his letter of 26 September 1781. He waxed so loquacious about the music to Act I on this occasion because he had earlier sent excerpts of it to his father, which he was anxious to explain as musician to musician. At this time he had also set to work on Act II, having completed another piece of 'Turkish' music (the duet 'Vivat, Bachus!' [B10]) and 'an aria' (probably either Blonde's [B6] or Pedrillo's [B9]).

Two musical additions were contemplated for this act. The first was another aria for Osmin, in line with the overall musical expansion of Fischer's role in the opera. In his reference to this projected aria Mozart cannot have meant 'O! wie will ich triumphiren' (No. 19), which was later added to Act III, since that aria eventually replaced an episode in the abduction ensemble, and at the time he wrote this letter Mozart still intended to set Bretzner's ensemble to music. Indeed, Mozart tells Leopold that this 'charming quintet, or rather finale' (B12) is to be moved to the end of Act II, and an entirely new intrigue will have to be manufactured to replace it at the beginning of Act III. This is the first mention we have of any departure from Bretzner's dramatic plan. Up to now, musical numbers had been added or created out of pre-existent dialogue, and Stephanie had been asked to change nothing in the construction of the plot.

The Gluck revival

Soon after this, Mozart learnt of another delay. Joseph's state chancellor, Prince Kaunitz, had already urged the emperor in July to give the grand duke and his wife 'a high idea of the power of this monarchy by every means possible' during their visit. With the observation '*chi più spende, meno spende*' Kaunitz suggested that His Majesty 'have brought from Italy, for example, three or four of the best voices in existence today to give a magnificent Italian opera seria'.[1] Eventually the court decided on a course of action which offered an even more eloquent and patriotic illustration of Vienna's position in the exalted spheres of serious opera – a production by the National Singspiel of Gluck's *Iphigénie en Tauride*, translated into German, and his *Alceste*, to be performed with the original Italian text by the German company.

On 6 October Mozart told his father that his new opera could not be performed until both of these Gluckian masterpieces had been presented, for they required all the energies of Adamberger and Fischer. With more time now than he had ever contemplated having, Mozart settled back to think through the project he had undertaken.

Leopold, meanwhile, had responded some time in early October to the music from the first act which Mozart had sent him. The loss of Leopold's remarks on this music is an unhappy one, for they elicited one of Mozart's most important epistolary ruminations on the relationship of music and poetry in opera:

Now about the text of the opera. – As far as Stephanie's work on it is concerned, you are admittedly correct. – Still, the poetry is wholly in keeping with the character of the foolish, coarse, and spiteful Osmin. – And I am aware that its metre is not the best – but it is so appropriate, and fits so well with my musical ideas (which were already parading around in my head beforehand), that I necessarily had to be happy with it; – and I would bet that in performance nothing will be missed. – As far as the poetry in the original work itself [i.e. Bretzner's libretto] is concerned, it is really nothing to sneeze at. – Belmonte's aria, 'O wie ängstlich, etc.,' could scarcely be better written for music. – Except for the 'hui' and 'kummer ruht in meinem Schoos' (for grief – can't rest), the aria really isn't bad; especially the first part. – And I really don't know – in an opera the poetry absolutely must be the obedient daughter of the music. – Why else are Italian comic operas popular everywhere? – considering how wretched their librettos are! – even in Paris – which I myself witnessed. – Because the music rules entirely in them – and when that is the case everything else is forgotten. – Certainly an opera must please all the more when the piece's plan is carefully worked out; the words, however, are written solely for the music and not stuck in for the sake of a miserable rhyme here and there (which doesn't contribute a thing, by God, to the value of a theatrical performance, whatever it may be, but in fact harms it instead) – or whole strophes, which ruin the entire conception of the composer. Verses are, it is true, the most indispensable thing for the music. – But rhyme – for rhyme's sake is the most harmful; – the gentlemen who operate so pedantically will always come to grief and the music along with them.

So the best thing is for a good composer who understands the theatre and has something of his own to contribute, to meet up with a clever poet, a true phoenix. – Then one need not worry about the applause of the ignorant. – Poets almost remind me of trumpeters with their journeyman's tricks! – If we composers were always to follow *our* rules so faithfully (which were perfectly fine at a time when no one knew any better), we would write music that is just as unsuitable as the librettos they write. –

Now I think I've chattered away to you enough about these silly things (13 October 1781).

This famous passage can be broken down into two parts. The first we can assume to be a point-by-point reply to remarks about the musical texts of Act I made in Leopold's lost letter of early October. Otherwise we would have to assume that Mozart mistakenly placed part of Constanze's first aria in Belmonte's 'O wie ängstlich' (see the sentence beginning 'Except for the "hui"'). Such an oversight is scarcely credible, for the whole letter breathes keen involvement with the texts on which Mozart had been labouring.

The second half of the passage is introduced by Mozart's well-known dictum about poetry playing the obedient daughter, and amounts to a spontaneous effusion on the problems occupying his mind as he studied the musical texts of Bretzner and Stephanie (which, we may notice, he distinguishes clearly). Concern here focuses exclusively on the poetry, not the spoken dialogue. References to Stephanie in other letters from this period make it clear that Mozart entertained a high opinion of his collaborator's dramatic skills. He no doubt left decisions concerning the dialogue in Stephanie's hands, and Stephanie, in turn, was happy to abide by what Bretzner had written – at least for the first act.

After the torrent of information and commentary on the music of Act I which Mozart provided for Leopold during September and October, his subsequent letters mention the opera less and less frequently and in little or no detail. In early November Stephanie finally had 'something ready' for Mozart, who in a letter of 3 November still speaks in terms of completing the opera quickly: two singers for Umlauf's rival production (*Das Irrlicht*) were ill, and Mozart hoped to steal a march on the National Singspiel's Kapellmeister.

Gluck's operas, meanwhile, lived up to general expectations as the artistic events of the season. *Iphigénie en Tauride*, translated by the young Viennese poet Johann Baptist von Alxinger, was produced on 23 October under Gluck's personal supervision, despite the composer's declining health. *Alceste* followed, in Italian, first at the Schönbrunn Palace Theatre in honour of the Russian visitors on 25 November, then at the Burgtheater. The National Singspiel, flushed with success, decided to follow up with a new production of Gluck's *Orfeo ed Euridice* on 31 December, with the part of Orfeo (originally written for the great castrato Guadagni) taken by Adamberger.

During this Gluck revival no other new opera was brought into production by the National Singspiel. Even after these three works were on the boards, only one further work was added to the repertory during the rest of the season (from New Year's Day to the beginning of Lent) – Umlauf's long-suffering *Das Irrlicht*, on 17 January 1782, shortly after the departure of the Russian visitors. It was all but lost in the shuffle, for between the introduction of *Iphigénie* and Shrove Tuesday Gluck's three operas and his opéra-comique *La Rencontre imprévue* monopolised the stage. For twenty-seven of the thirty-eight nights on which operas were given by the National Singspiel during this period, one of these four works was given. (*Das Irrlicht* hung on, however, and soon became one of the most popular German operas of the decade in Vienna.)

Not surprisingly, Mozart's hopes of producing his opera with any speed had quickly evaporated in late 1781. For the winter season other commitments and difficulties preoccupied his mind – not the least of which was his decision to marry Constanze Weber, a development that generated unprecedented tension between Wolfgang and Leopold.

On 30 January Mozart reassured his father that his German opera was not dormant, but owing to Gluck's operas and to 'many very necessary alterations in the poetry' it would not be given until after Easter. What were these 'very necessary alterations'? Mozart does not tell us. But the very phrase bears witness to the fact that, once the opportunity to rethink seriously the opera's musical shape had presented itself, Mozart and Stephanie introduced substantial changes in the portion yet to be composed – that is, in much of Act II and in all of Act III. In contrast, Act I, set to music under severe time pressure, had preserved even in its final form all five of Bretzner's original musical items in its seven numbers (see again Table 2).

Mozart's letters say virtually nothing about the changes he and Stephanie made in the last two acts of Bretzner's plan. We glean from his correspondence only a few dates: on 8 May he played all of Act II for the Countess Thun-Hohenstein, one of his warmest admirers among the Viennese aristocracy; on 30 May he played all of Act III for her; and on 3 June the finished opera was finally put into rehearsal.

If we glance forward at the synopsis provided in Chapter 4, we can form an idea of the kinds of adjustments Mozart and Stephanie made in the last two acts. Some of the additions and alterations continue the pattern established earlier for the first act: the duet for Osmin and Blonde (No. 9), the recitative to lend greater expressive force to Constanze's aria 'Traurigkeit' (B7), a cheery aria for Blonde after her scene with Pedrillo (No. 12), yet another aria for Belmonte near the end of Act II (No. 15) which replaces a few lines of dialogue, and in Act III an added aria for Fischer to close the abduction scene (No. 19). They disturb nothing in the original plan, and we may assume with some confidence that, like all the changes in Act I, each one came at Mozart's behest.

Other additions are of a different order, however. In Act II Constanze's *aria di bravura* 'Martern aller Arten' required three new scenes from Stephanie and, what is more, the presentation of a wholly unexplored side of Constanze's personality. We shall deal with this most celebrated and problematic of the opera's arias later in Chapter 5. The great quartet at the end of the act, justly admired by everyone who writes about *Die Entführung aus dem Serail*, posed far fewer problems than Constanze's aria. Stephanie found the incident upon which he based this episode already at hand in Bretzner's dialogue.

The decision to dismantle the extensive quintet Bretzner had written for the abduction scene near the beginning of Act III was forced on Stephanie and Mozart once they realised that it could not be moved to the end of Act II.[2] In Berlin, perhaps, one could still put a number which was a finale in everything but name wherever the dramatic logic called for it, but Vienna lay too much in the thrall of the patterns of opera buffa. Stephanie's task in turning it back into dialogue and closed numbers was not a difficult one. He could easily be persuaded to write a substitute text for Belmonte's 'Welch ängstliches Beben' (an aria which formed the first section of the original abduction quintet, B12), because it duplicated almost exactly the sentiments of Belmonte's 'O wie ängstlich' in Act I. Stephanie knew the rules for treating important singers like Adamberger, singers who demanded arias which would show all sides of their voices to greatest advantage. Pedrillo's Romanze 'In Mohrenland' (No. 18) presented no problem at all – it was already there, embedded in Bretzner's quintet.

Up to the last scene of the opera, in sum, Stephanie had made only one significant change in Bretzner's dramatic plan – the added scenes around Constanze's 'Martern aller Arten' in Act II. He was to make one more: at the moment when the captured lovers are brought before Selim, Stephanie jettisoned the model he had been following so closely and substituted a new denouement. The scene introduces a new dimension to the character of Selim, a spoken role, so musical considerations can have had little bearing on the substitution. Here, it would appear, Stephanie offered his sole original contribution to the literary edifice he had received from Bretzner.

Stephanie's hand

What can we say about the respective roles Mozart and Stephanie played in creating the major departures from Bretzner? Compared with an opera such as *Idomeneo*, the documentary resources necessary to answer such a question are comparatively few. No preliminary sketches for the opera survive save for an abandoned effort at composing the action quintet encompassing the abduction scene near the beginning of Act III. The autograph score represents the sole musical authority for the opera as it was completed and performed in July of 1782.

Mozart's letters on the *Entführung*, although of incontestably pre-eminent value as witnesses to his evolving aesthetic of opera in the early 1780s, deal exclusively with changes worked on Act I of Bretzner's libretto, which are on the whole less interesting than the alterations to Acts II and III just discussed. Two other documents, none the less, shed at least a little light on Stephanie's role in the opera's revision. The first is the original edition itself of *Die Entführung aus dem Serail*, issued in July of 1782 under the auspices of the 'Logenmeister', as was normal in conjunction with the première of a new opera at the Burgtheater. Plate 1 reproduces the title page of this publication.

If we compare the portions which Stephanie took directly from Bretzner as they appear in this edition with the same texts in the original printed version (*Belmont und Constanze*), we observe a remarkable correlation, not only in the words but also in orthography, punctuation and the disposition of the verses of the musical

Die
Entführung aus dem Serail.

Ein Singspiel
in drey Aufzügen,
nach Bretznern
frey bearbeitet, und für das k. k. Nationalhoftheater eingerichtet.

In Musik gesetzt
vom
Herrn Mozart.

Aufgeführt im k. k. Nationalhoftheater.

Wien,
zu finden beym Logenmeister, 1782.

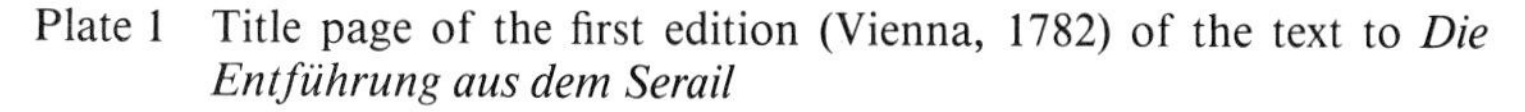

Plate 1 Title page of the first edition (Vienna, 1782) of the text to *Die Entführung aus dem Serail*

texts. Even stage directions are taken over unchanged. There is only one plausible explanation for this: Stephanie handed over to the imperial printer a copy of Bretzner's libretto itself, with his own added musical texts and scenes written out separately. It was only natural, therefore, that he made no mention of his own name on the title page or anywhere else in the libretto, but simply inserted the phrase 'freely adapted after Herr Bretzner'.

The second document bearing on Stephanie's conception of his part in 'freely adapting' Bretzner's libretto appeared a decade after the première of *Die Entführung aus dem Serail* – the collected edition of his German comic operas, issued in 1792. Stephanie did not include the *Entführung*, or any of his other adaptations of Bretzner's librettos, in this volume. He did include, however, an interesting preface[3] in which he discusses several problems plaguing German comic opera, notably a lack of good singers and of good original texts.

The former can be easily remedied with higher salaries, he notes, but the second is not so easy to correct: 'Certainly good librettos have been written now and then,' he admits, 'but they seldom had the proper form of a Singspiel and usually they had to be revised, because the composers for these librettos could not and would not set them as they stood.' Stephanie's next sentence makes it clear that he is thinking of Bretzner's popular librettos of the early 1780s: 'And so I had to rework *Die Entführung aus dem Serail* for Mozart, *Das Irrlicht* for Umlauf, and *Das wütende Heer* for Ruprecht.'

Stephanie goes on to outline the rules a good opera ought to follow, rules he derived 'from the many translations of operas which I furnished, from association with and guidance from the composers for whom I wrote, and finally from six years of directing the opera with the Royal Imperial Court Theatre at Vienna'. He proposes a dozen specific points to keep in mind when creating a libretto. If we bring these to bear on the final text of *Die Entführung aus dem Serail*, we sense at once the compromises inherent in this work between the primitive conception of German opera current in the 1770s and the paradigm Stephanie was to propose in 1792:

Stephanie, 'Preface' (1792)	*Die Entführung (1782)*
1 18 to 24 numbers	21 numbers
2 divided properly into arias and 'concerted pieces'	14 arias, 7 ensembles and 2 choruses
3 begin with an ensemble	begins with an 'arietta'

4	end each act with an action finale including all principals	only Act II has a finale, and it contains inner rather than outer action
5	only seldom should more than two arias appear together	Act II: four in a row Act III: three in a row
6	consecutive arias should not be sung by the same person	Constanze sings two demanding arias in a row (Nos. 10 & 11)
7	thereafter a duet or trio should form a section	Nos. 2 and 9 do so (both added by Stephanie), plus the ensembles ending Acts I and II
8	at least three arias and a duet or trio for the main voices	Belmonte, Constanze and Osmin are so served; Pedrillo and Blonde have only two arias
9	numbers should not follow one another too closely	only a line or two of dialogue between numbers at the start of Act I and some other spots
10	put nothing absolutely necessary to the intrigue in the musical numbers	observed in both versions
11	few singing roles so as to use only good singers	only five, with Selim a spoken role
12	avoid choruses	two, both for the same group

Most of these points are self-explanatory. Some are followed scrupulously in the *Entführung*, others are not, and in most cases these deviations go back to Bretzner's original plan. A clear instance of Stephanie's stronger operatic sensitivity is his use of musical numbers to close off a scene (almost always marked dramatically with the exit of a character). Bretzner had included nine arias in his original version, none of them exit arias. Stephanie decided to retain seven of these, but he also added six new arias, and four of them are exit arias. The duet of Osmin and Blonde in Act II functions in the same way.

It may be objected – and with good reason – that we have been over-charitable in assigning to Stephanie alterations that may well have come from the composer. To see what a difference Mozart's involvement made in the creation of the *Entführung* we need only examine the activities of his Viennese contemporaries. Umlauf's *Das Irrlicht*, already mentioned several times, offers an unusually close basis for comparison – both texts are by Bretzner and both were adapted by Stephanie for the National Singspiel at nearly the same time and with several of the same singers in mind. Bretzner's original libretto (*Der Irrwisch*) had contained a healthy thirty-one numbers. Stephanie omitted five of them, left twenty-one exactly as they were, and made only minor verbal adjustments in four others. He rewrote one aria for Fischer and, in his only substantial exertion of poetic energy, substituted a finale at the end of Act II for two duets and intervening dialogue. Such minor tinkering scarcely bears comparison with what Mozart had him do to *Belmont und Constanze.*

We might ask another question here as well: who among the local composers who contributed to the National Singspiel went on to write opera buffa for the Italian company which superseded the German one at the Burgtheater in 1783? Only two – Mozart and Salieri. For both these composers, the great ease with which they returned from German to Italian comic opera was matched by great unease in the alliance which their lone German operas for the National Singspiel had struck between spoken and musical traditions. Mozart's insistence throughout the genesis of *Die Entführung aus dem Serail* that music's prerogatives not be short-changed had to make its peace with the hybrid nature of opera with spoken dialogue. Only to a certain degree could a libretto conceived in a tradition beholden to the overpowering demands of spoken drama be adapted to the musical stage, even to one with the cultural loyalties of the Viennese National Singspiel.

3 *Oriental opera*

Islam and its believers have never been perceived with either objectivity or indifference by the West. Several perceptions and misperceptions, codified during the Middle Ages, enjoyed remarkable longevity in Western attitudes. Europeans recognised Islam as one of the three great monotheistic religions but also as 'the sum of all heresy', in the words of Norman Daniel. 'The two most important aspects of Muhammad's life, Christians believed, were his sexual license and his use of force to establish his religion.'[1]

Over the past millennium the relationship of the West and Islamic culture has moved in a vast swing of the pendulum from an initial period of Moorish expansionism, through a lengthy decline ending with the military impotence of the Ottoman Empire at the end of the seventeenth century, into a modern phase of Western imperialism and colonialism, which began with Napoleon's invasion of Egypt in 1798.

In the areas of literature, theatre, travel and fashion the eighteenth century turned again and again to the East, and usually with a strong sense of ambivalence. On the one hand, what W. Daniel Wilson[2] has called the medieval 'Crusade mentality' perpetuated in European minds the image of the sabre-wielding Muslim long after the practical military danger posed by the Turks had evaporated. At the same time, most of the leading writers of the Enlightenment turned specifically to the cultures of the East to create heroes directly counter to this popular image. Thus there co-existed in eighteenth-century Europe two contrary paradigms of the Eastern world in 'high' and 'low' culture, directly reflected in Selim and Osmin and in their predecessors on European stages.

Bretzner and the vogue Oriental opera

As a military presence the Turks offered a source of direct concern only to the Habsburg Empire and to Russia, both of whom went to war with them during the last half of the century. There is no doubt that, even in the 1780s under Joseph II, Austria harboured unhappy memories of the Turkish siege of Vienna in 1683, and that some fears still lingered over the potential threat posed by the Ottoman Empire. But we must remember that the text of Mozart's opera was conceived not by Stephanie at Vienna but by a businessman living and writing at Leipzig, who must have regarded current events involving Turkey with mild indifference. Not, however, the Oriental world as it was portrayed and imagined in the century's literature, drama, and opera. No matters of state guided this tradition; rather, it fed on the reports – increasingly numerous – of soldiers, travellers and traders, and on Oriental literature itself.

Western theatrical representations had already developed a set of character types and plot structures for plays and operas set in Moorish or Eastern lands. Some of these works are purely exotic – that is, they not only take place in the Orient, they also include exclusively Eastern personages. The best-known of the group, Grétry's *Zémire et Azor* (1771), also illustrates the penchant for music, magic and the supernatural in this strain.

More often, however, Oriental drama and opera of the eighteenth century transported a set of Westerners to some part of the Eastern world. The two features of Muhammad's life for which he was traditionally reviled in the West – sensuality and cruelty – were projected on to the Muslims peopling these works. Usually these ingredients brought several others in their train: the harem as a part of a general garden of earthly delights; escape as the only hope for the European beauty brought into such a seraglio by capture or purchase; wholesale threats of torture and death; and an utter inability on the part of the Muslims to comprehend European mores and manners.

No single work has been isolated among the Oriental operas preceding *Belmont und Constanze* as Bretzner's direct source or model, although various scholars have proposed a number of works from English, German and Italian traditions.[3] The libretto is better regarded from a less narrow perspective as one among a clutch of texts drawing on a constellation of plot elements and characters associated with the East.

Writers have pointed out parallels to the plot of *Belmont und Constanze* as far back as Menander and Plautus,[4] attesting to the venerability of such stock features as a recognition scene involving a father and a captive who turns out to be his son, or the contrasting of the lowly, visceral urges of a slave with the high-minded actions of his master.

Among eighteenth-century European dramatic traditions, those of the English stage offer the least direct affinities with Bretzner's libretto, although many writers have echoed Edward Dent's claim that it 'was imitated from an English comic opera, *The Captive*, performed in 1769 with music by Dibdin and others'. Isaac Bickerstaffe created this two-act text from the comic sub-plot in John Dryden's tragedy *Don Sebastian* (1689), in which a young Portuguese, bought by an Algerian Mufti as a present for his wife, escapes with his master's daughter and his jewels, the fruits of the Mufti's extorting and embezzling. Bickerstaffe altered several features to bring the tale into line with the theatrical sensibilities of his day. The hero, now Spanish rather than Portuguese, completely loses his opportunistic concupiscence (in Dryden he tries to seduce the Mufti's daughter forthwith; she, however, intends to marry him and become a Christian and warns him not to try 'fing'ring your Rents before-hand'). Bickerstaffe's callow counterpart is also no longer a slave but is working in the Cadi's (Mufti's) garden until a ship can take him to Spain. Human defects and excesses reside solely in the Easterners. The Cadi remains Dryden's venal Moor, ever ready to flay and impale those who cross him, while his wife tries hard to tempt the young Spaniard to her bed.

Bickerstaffe appropriated another comic opera he created for Dibdin, *The Sultan, or a Peep into the Seraglio* (1775), from Favart's *Soliman II.* of 1761. Several writers have noticed the proximity of Favart's saucy Frenchwoman Roxelane (an Englishwoman in Bickerstaffe's version) to Blonde. But Roxelane uses her wiles to secure the Grand Sultan for herself alone and even obtains co-regency over all of Turkey, while Blonde's commitments are to her personal liberty and to her fiancé Pedrillo.

Recently, Rudolf Angermüller brought to light an obscure French play, dated 1755, *Les Époux esclaves ou Bastien et Bastienne à Alger.*[5] Osman, commander of the Algerian navy, endeavours to win the heart of Bastienne, a French slave brought by capture to his household together with her husband Bastien. While Osman wrestles with his extreme emotions of love and hate, Bastien plots his assassination with the other French slaves. Bastienne divulges the plot and saves Osman's life; he in turn rewards the couple with their freedom. It is questionable whether Bretzner could have known anything of this little one-act drama, which survives only in a single manuscript copy in Paris. The parallels with *Belmont und Constanze* indicate, none the less, how the elements of shipwrecked Iberian lovers, a powerful Muslim and his underling, an escape plot and a generous deed to bring about the happy ending came quickly to many writers contemplating a drama about Europeans thrust into the Islamic world.

Italian dramatists and librettists, although fond of the Orient, tended away from the exploitation of East–West confrontations.[6] An exception is a *dramma serio-buffo per musica* which Walter Preibisch has proposed as one of the most direct influences on Bretzner, Gaetano Martinelli's *La schiava liberata*, composed by Jommelli and performed before the ducal court of Karl Eugen in 1768 at Ludwigsburg. Selim, the proud admiral of the Algerian navy, has fallen passionately in love with his captive Dorimene, the fiancée of Don Garzia, a Spanish nobleman. Selim's father Solimano, the Bey of Algeria, has arranged a marriage between his son and Elmira, the daughter of the rich Circassian Albumazar. Selim stubbornly refuses to give up Dorimene, however. Complications arise when Albumazar becomes infatuated with Dorimene's servant Giulietta, herself in love with Don Garzia's servant Pallottino, and when Don Garzia himself arrives from Spain to negotiate the release of Dorimene and the two servants. Albumazar is twice exposed to ridicule – first, when he tries to visit Giulietta while dressed as a woman, and second, when he attempts a hopelessly inept impersonation of the French consul. Selim, meanwhile, spurns Elmira again and again, terrorises the cowardly Pallottino into helping in his pursuit of Dorimene, and in consequence becomes the object of an assassination attempt by Elmira, foiled by Dorimene (an episode Martinelli borrowed from Goldoni's *La sposa persana* of 1753). After a last wild attack on the departing lovers, Selim finally yields Dorimene to Don Garzia and accepts the much-maligned Elmira.

The import of *La schiava liberata* for Bretzner's libretto is partly circumstantial. In 1777, nine years after Jommelli's version, Joseph Schuster set Martinelli's text for the buffo singers at the Dresden court, a production which probably did not escape Bretzner's notice in nearby Leipzig. Yet the points of contact between the two librettos dwindle in their significance beside the many divergences, which reflect two disparate operatic traditions. The lovers can be equated, as Preibisch equates them, only because they are stock types.

Albumazar has little in common with Osmin beyond his ill-starred passion and his swift recourse to violent threats, traits he shares with many other Turks in theatre and literature.

Martinelli's Selim, without direct parallel in *Belmont und Constanze* or any other Turkish opera, incorporates these same two features in a towering struggle which only the accents of serious opera could articulate. Martinelli and Jommelli created this part specifically for the great castrato Giuseppe Aprile. Bretzner could in no way entertain such a conception in his German opera for the minions of Döbbelin's German company at Berlin, just as he had to do without the frequent scene changes and opportunities for spectacle which Martinelli knew the Württemberg court wanted and was willing to pay for.

Germany not only welcomed many Oriental operas from abroad, it also produced a spate of new ones in the decade leading up to *Belmont und Constanze.* Many drew directly on French models. The Mannheim publisher Christian Friedrich Schwan translated Chamfort's one-act afterpiece *Le Marchand de Smyrne* when it appeared in 1770, then turned this into a libretto for young Georg Joseph Vogler a year later; it became *Der Kaufmann von Smyrna*, and was set by several other German composers soon after. In this short action the Turk Hassan and his wife purchase the freedom of the French couple Dorval and Amalie from the rapacious slave-dealer Kaled. The deed is one of repayment rather than generosity, for Hassan himself had been freed once by Dorval under similar circumstances.

An original libretto from 1774, *Der Bassa von Tunis*, which the actor–playwright Karl Friedrich Henisch put together for his friend, the Czech composer Franz Andreas Holly, shares only incidental features with other Oriental operas. The Pasha in this tale is actually an Italian woman who lost her lover Alzindor while he was defending her from pirates. In despair she disguised herself as a man and fought so fiercely for the Grand Sultan that he made her Pasha of Tunis. Later she learnt that Alzindor was still alive. To test his constancy she wrote to him, pretending to be a slave in the Pasha's household. He turns up among a group of captives and proves his loyalty by trying to free her.

The libretto closest to *Belmont und Constanze* was created at virtually the same time, in the Rhineland, by the actor–dramatist–theatre manager Gustav Friedrich Wilhelm Grossmann. It is *Adelheit von Veltheim*, written for the composer Christian Gottlob

Neefe. In September of 1780 Grossmann dispatched the finished text to the Leipzig publisher Dyk, and a month later Bretzner wrote an open letter to a local theatrical journal in which he recorded his amazement that he and Grossmann had 'by chance pursued almost the identical path'. *Belmont und Constanze*, he added, had been sent to André in July, a fact corroborated by another writer in a later issue.[7]

Bretzner's claim to innocence of any plagiary seems genuine. Thus *Adelheit von Veltheim* illustrates again how the popular motifs of Oriental opera and drama could be configured in quite similar ways by dramatists working independently within the same theatrical tradition.

Pasha Selim and the figure of the noble Turk

With only a few exceptions, the comic and serious Westerners in these Oriental operas represent stock types that see use again and again. The Turks, nearly always male, are far more intriguing and more variable from opera to opera. The ambiguity in Western apprehensions of Islamic culture, stressed by Wilson, resonates in the Muslims of these operas. In character they range from the unstintingly admirable – Hassan in *Der Kaufmann von Smyrna* or Achmet in *Adelheit von Veltheim* – to the irredeemably nasty – Kaled in *Der Kaufmann von Smyrna* or the Cadi in *The Captive*.

But more often the Turk appears as a mixture of the benign and the malevolent, of the dangerous and the risible. The social message these works embody is similarly mixed. Sometimes these Easterners function as external vantage points from which to fire criticisms at the failings of the West – a technique which goes back to Montesquieu's *Lettres persanes* of 1721. But the trade can also run in the opposite direction. As an example, in *Adelheit von Veltheim* Miss Flour fairly bristles over Muhammad's having granted a man dominion over a dozen women or more. 'You cannot imagine,' she tells the others, 'how such a thing inflames me – a free-born Englishwoman.' In *Der Bassa von Tunis*, on the other hand, one Moorish beauty in the Pasha's harem observes drily that European men are allowed one wife by law 'and secretly they have even more than our Muslims'.

The most interesting Turks in these operas are those thwarted by the one major theme we can extract from all of them – the conflicting sexual mores and values of East and West. Nearly always the Muslim in question has had the misfortune to fall in love with a European captive. The Western stereotypes of Islamic violence and sexual licence, which both intimidated and fascinated the European mind, inevitably lose their power and terror once the Muslim is coerced into acting and thinking like a European lover. At the end of a long line of such lovers stands Pasha Selim in *Die Entführung aus dem Serail.*

Bretzner's Selim is the least developed and least significant of the six principals in his drama. He appears only twice and does not sing at all. He does, however, add a new twist to the operatic conception of the Oriental potentate, for Selim is not really a Turk by birth but a renegade. We never learn the reason for which he forswore Christianity and the West, since Bretzner seems to have introduced the idea as a necessary preparation for the revelation of Selim as Belmonte's father. But a secondary benefit accrues, for the concept helps explain Selim's comportment toward Constanze. In Act I Pedrillo tells Belmonte that the renegade Selim 'has retained so much delicacy as to force none of his wives to his love'. Bretzner downplays Selim's polygamy by not allowing his other wives to appear on stage, as they do in Grossmann's *Adelheit von Veltheim.* Nor does Selim ever directly threaten Constanze – he simply reminds her of the power he holds over her. Only the betrayal of his trust and goodwill by all four of the lovers drives him in Act III to order them all to be strangled.

Stephanie expanded Bretzner's Pasha into a more complex and interesting character. In the added scene with Constanze in Act II Selim intensifies the tone set by their interaction in the preceding act, urging his suit with a veiled threat of tortures should Constanze refuse him. But then he reacts to her 'Martern aller Arten' with a monologue of humane sensibility: he now recognises the futility of threats as well as pleas in his efforts to win her heart, and upon recovering from his astonishment at her outburst he charitably ascribes her open defiance to the workings of despair.

The capital gesture which etches Stephanie's Selim most sharply in our minds is his magnanimous forgiveness of the lovers in the last scene of the opera. Stephanie undertook this change in Bretzner's original ending not because he found the latter improbable – the chances of Belmonte's being the son of Selim's arch-enemy are no better than those of his being Selim's own son – but for the edifying example it enabled Selim to set.

In a review of the première of *Die Entführung aus dem Serail,* Johann Friedrich Schink objected to the Pasha's generous deed in forgiving his enemy – a nobler motivation for freeing the lovers than

Bretzner's recognition scheme, he admits, 'but also – as is always the case with such noble acts – incomparably more unnatural'.[8] Why, then, did Stephanie trouble to include it, especially in view of his general policy of preserving as much as possible of Bretzner's original text? Schink offered an answer:

> In general these endless acts of magnanimity are a wretched thing, and in fashion on scarcely a single stage any more save the one here. And one can almost be sure that such a work containing handsome feats of magnanimity, generosity, recognition, and forgiveness will make a great splash, even if these things are brought about in the most unnatural way.

The word Schink invoked here, 'unnatural', saw much use at the time in discussions of opera seria. Under Joseph the genre was quite out of fashion at Vienna, but it served as the well-spring of such culminating musical moments as the Act III recitative and duet of Belmonte and Constanze. Something of this operatic tradition guides the behaviour of Selim as well. In the Metastasian canon a final gesture of forgiveness and clemency such as Selim's amounted to a cliché.

Yet another tradition also seems to be at work. Upon first confronting the lovers and their deceptions, Selim fairly seethes with thoughts of Mosaic requital, of an eye for an eye, of visiting the sins of the father upon the son. He emerges as something approaching an imitation of Christ, forgiving his enemies and even seeing to their safe passage home.[9]

Behind this Biblical parallel there lies a pattern established by several earlier operatic Turks and already followed by Selim in his added scenes with Constanze in Act II, an instinctive inclination to violent action which reflection transforms into self-control, resignation and generosity. One catches only a hint of this in the last finale of *La schiava liberata*, where the hot-headed young Selim's yielding to necessity appears dramatically forced and psychologically abrupt, as is often the case in opera buffa texts of the period. Similar situations in French and German traditions capitalise on the usefulness of spoken dialogue for fashioning more careful and convincing scenes. The Sultan in *La Rencontre imprévue* and the Pasha in *Adelheit von Veltheim*, both far less dagger-happy than Martinelli's Selim, grant freedom and forgiveness to the intercepted lovers in scenes that must not have been lost on Stephanie when he revised *Belmont und Constanze*.

Bretzner had improved upon these earlier models in one important way – he established a source for Selim's ambivalence by making him a renegade. On one front, this offered Western audiences the comfort of interpreting Selim's magnanimity as a happy residue of his Occidental upbringing, and his occasional tendency to torture and violence as a foreign, specifically Turkish trait. But it was Stephanie who also saw in Selim's Western past an opportunity to establish him in our minds as a sympathetic character, as one who has suffered losses: 'It was because of your father, this barbarian,' he tells Belmonte, 'that I was forced to leave my homeland. His unbending greed tore a love from me whom I valued above my own life. He deprived me of rank, fortune, everything. In short, he destroyed all my happiness.'

Bretzner had no doubt had his reasons for conceiving of Selim more as a father than as an absolute ruler. Stephanie, for his part, could not fail to think of Joseph, the guiding spirit behind the creation and development of the National Singspiel. In contrast, what did Bretzner care about the benevolent despots either in his own home or at Berlin, for whose German theatre he wrote *Belmont und Constanze*? The Elector of Saxony had by 1780 lost what little interest he ever had in German opera, and Frederick the Great had always regarded it with utter disdain.

Then, too, the German stages in Saxony, Prussia and the rest of north and central Germany were almost all in private hands and served largely non-court audiences. For them Bretzner's familial tableau of recognition, reunion and rejoicing formed a fitting and familiar conclusion. Stephanie's Selim, in contrast, presented Burgtheater audiences with a statesman rather than father. Ultimately, he is a ruler of the opera seria stamp, and this is perhaps why Schink found him 'unnatural'. The suddenness and extent of his magnanimity form an essential trait of the model monarchs created by Metastasio. And in the same tradition, the new closing number of *Die Entführung aus dem Serail* allowed Mozart to shower Stephanie's Pasha Selim with not only the gratitude of those he has pardoned, but also the encomia of those over whom he will continue to rule.

4 *Synopsis*

Most synopses of *Die Entführung aus dem Serail* are based on the text printed for the première of Mozart's opera or on some later modification of this text. The one which follows presents the content not only of this principal source (referred to here as 'Vienna, 1782') but also of Bretzner's published libretto as Mozart received it in July 1781 from Stephanie ('Leipzig, 1781'). Where Stephanie altered or supplemented his model we summarise his version in the left-hand column and Bretzner's original text to the right. The usefulness of distinguishing these two editions will become apparent in the next chapter.

Cast of characters

Person	*First Interpreter, voice*
Selim, a Pasha	Dominik Joseph Jautz, spoken role
Constanze, the beloved of Belmonte	Caterina Cavalieri, soprano
Blonde, Constanze's maid	Therese Teyber, soprano
Belmonte	Johann Valentin Adamberger, tenor
Pedrillo, Belmonte's servant, and supervisor of the Pasha's gardens	Josef Valentin Adamberger, tenor
Osmin, supervisor of the Pasha's country house	Johann Ignaz Ludwig Fischer, bass
Klaas, a boatsman	
Janissaries, slaves, guards	

PLACE: The scene is the country estate of the Pasha.

ACT I

Stage setting: *A plaza in front of the Pasha's palace on the seashore.* A three-part overture introduces the opera's Oriental milieu with all the traits typical of eighteenth-century 'Turkish' music, a topic to be discussed in Chapter 5. In between the overture's outer sections – exposition and abbreviated reprise – appears a minor-mode adumbration of Belmonte's opening C major Lied. It encapsulates exquisitely the mixture of hesitancy and lyricism that dominates his personality. The overture's minor-mode version, more languorous and plangent, seems to suggest Belmonte's many months of fruitless searching for Constanze, and thus acts as a foil which brightens the hopes expressed in the major-mode aria.

Scene 1

Vienna, 1782
No. 1 Aria (Belmonte: *Hier soll ich dich denn sehen*).
The young Spanish nobleman Belmonte, after many sorrows withstood in the name of love, finds himself at last at the place where he hopes to find his beloved, Constanze.

Leipzig, 1781
Monologue (expressing the same sentiments, but in somewhat lengthier prose).

Monologue: But how is he to gain entrance to the palace in order to speak with her?

Scene 2

The old Turk Osmin appears with a ladder and begins picking figs.

Vienna, 1782
No. 2 Lied and Duet
(Osmin, Belmonte: *Wer ein Liebchen hat gefunden*).

Leipzig, 1781
(Aria and spoken dialogue.)

As he works, Osmin sings a strophic song about how to hold on to a lover who is honest and true. Belmonte tries to get his attention between stanzas with questions about whether this might be Pasha Selim's palace. Osmin pretends to ignore him, but does none the less alter the tone of strophes two and three so that they point directly to the intentions he imputes to this unwelcome young stranger. In the first stanza, he sings that one must make life as sweet as can be for one's sweetheart, but then in the next one he advises locking her up, safe from the young roués who are always prowling about. Especially in the moonlight, one must be careful, he concludes in the third: one of these dandies will lure the little fool away, and then you may as well kiss fidelity goodbye.

Vienna, 1782	*Leipzig, 1781*
[Duet] Belmonte puts an end to Osmin's song. He has questions in need of answering. Osmin, impatient to leave, acknowledges that this is Pasha Selim's palace and that he is in his service, but the mention of Pedrillo kindless his ire.	**Dialogue** (virtually the same, but in less detail and in prose).
An argument develops over Pedrillo's merits. Osmin tries to leave again, but Belmonte strikes out on another tack. Osmin, however, interrupts his manoeuvre and states his suspicions about Belmonte's designs on the Pasha's harem. A shouting match ensues; it ends with Osmin's driving Belmonte off.	Osmin accuses Belmonte of being as roguish a foreigner as Pedrillo and a spy into the bargain. Belmonte seeks to soften Osmin's hostility with a douceur, but receives only imprecations and a rude ejection.

Mozart up to this point has exercised complete control over the unfolding of the drama, with the result that the conventional dramatic exposition has been somewhat delayed. He could not resist, either, amplifying the next scene too with an exit aria for Osmin, already more than amply provided for and now transformed into the most consummate musical personality yet created in comic opera. (This aria and the preceding duet are discussed in connexion with Mozart's 'Turkish' style in Chapter 5, pp. 68–71.)

Scene 3

Dialogue: Osmin mutters to himself about the villain Pedrillo, who does nothing but skulk around Osmin's wives. Should he ever collar him, Pedrillo will pay dearly. And were it not that Pedrillo had wormed his way into the Pasha's good graces, he would have been hanged a long time ago. Pedrillo comes and asks if the Pasha has returned, and if Osmin has picked the figs Pedrillo had requested. Osmin sets about abusing him at once – he is a damned parasite, a stinking, thieving spy, insufferable and fit to be throttled.

Vienna, 1782

No. 3 Aria (Osmin: *Solche hergelaufne Laffen*)
Osmin cannot stand such puppies, always after women, always spying. But he knows their tricks: they'll have to get up very early to fool him. And he'll not rest until he sees Pedrillo put to death.
Dialogue: Pedrillo protests that he has done nothing to Osmin. He has a hangdog face, Osmin replies:
Coda to No. 3: He runs through a list of the tortures, mutilations, and methods of execution awaiting Pedrillo. Exit Osmin.

Leipzig, 1781

Exit Osmin.

Scene 4

Dialogue: Pedrillo is relieved to be rid of such a mistrustful, spiteful misanthrope. A happy surprise befalls him: his master Belmonte appears. Pedrillo is elated that one of his letters found its way to him. Is Constanze yet living? Yes, and hopefully still for Belmonte. Pedrillo explains that, after their capture by pirates, the Pasha Selim bought all three of them – Constanze, himself and his Blonde. They were brought here, and Constanze has become Selim's chosen beloved. The worst has not yet come to pass, however. Selim is a renegade, and has retained enough of his Western delicacy that he will compel the love of none of his wives. As far as Pedrillo knows he is still playing the unanswered suitor. But God knows how things stand with Blonde. Selim made a gift of her to Osmin, the Pasha's favourite, his spy, and the paragon of all rascals. Luckily Pedrillo, too, stands in the Pasha's favour, thanks to his gardening skills. In fact, he can remain in the garden when one of Selim's wives walks there and can even speak to her – something no other male is allowed to do. Does Constanze still love Belmonte? Pedrillo is surprised that he can even ask such a question. They should be thinking instead of how to escape. Belmonte says he has a ship ready, but Pedrillo replies that they need to secure the women first, which will require some cunning. The Pasha is to return any minute from a pleasure trip on the water. Pedrillo will present Belmonte to him as a talented architect, for along with gardening, architecture is one of the Pasha's hobby-horses. He warns Belmonte to control himself, for Constanze will be with Selim. Pedrillo leaves.

Scene 5

No. 4 Recitative and Aria (Belmonte: *Constanze. . .O wie ängstlich*) The thought of seeing Constanze again fills Belmonte with anxiety and ardour. Already he shivers and reels, his breast swells. As he imagines hearing her whisper and sigh his cheeks grow warm and fear seizes him.

Perhaps the most eloquent thing in this great portrait of Belmonte (which we shall treat at greater length later) is the brief recitative Mozart set to 'Constanze! Constanze! To see you again!' – a line Bretzner had intended to be spoken. Verbally and psychologically this passage mediates between the preceding dialogue and the private lyric world built out of Belmonte's hopes and fears in the aria proper.
Dialogue: Pedrillo rushes back in. The Pasha is approaching, and Belmonte must hide.

Scene 6

No. 5a March

The Pasha and Constanze arrive in a pleasure boat. Another boat carrying Janissary musicians lands ahead of them. They arrange themselves on the shore.

Gerhard Croll has published in the Neue Mozart-Ausgabe an apparently authentic march written by Mozart for this spot, although missing in the autograph score. One listens in vain to hear it played, however, in subsequent recordings and performances. At all events, some such music for an on-stage wind band must occur here for the necessary stage business involving the Janissary musicians. For the orchestra in the pit to assume this role (the ritornello of the Chorus of Janissaries being the common choice) goes against eighteenth-century custom.

No. 5b Chorus of Janissaries (Chorus: *Singt dem grossen Bassa Lieder*)
The chorus sings a paean of joy and praise for their master, bidding the cooling breeze to blow on him, the waves to grow peaceful, and choruses from on high to sing the joy of love into his heart. Exeunt Janissaries.

Scene 7

Dialogue: Selim sees that Constanze's sorrow is impervious to her charming surroundings, the enchantments of music, and his tender love for her. He could deal cruelly with her and enforce her love, he observes, but he would rather have herself to thank for her heart. He has given her more freedom than all his other wives, so deep is his love, and he prizes her as his only one. She admires his generosity toward her, but fears that what prevents her loving him will incur his hatred. Entreating his forgiveness in advance, she explains.
No. 6 Aria (Constanze: *Ach, ich liebte*)
Once she loved happily, truly, and with her whole heart; love's pain was unknown to her. But how quickly her joy dissolved: separation has now brought tears to her eyes and care to her breast.

Constanze's introductory aria provided the subject for Mozart's now aphoristic reference to Caterina Cavalieri's 'geläufige Gurgel' ('I've sacrificed Constanze's aria a little to the flexible throat of Mlle. Cavalieri' – letter of 26 September 1781). It is easy to share the composer's misgivings, for the aria itself is far less flexible than the two Constanze sings back-to-back in Act II. None the less, it is not without its charms and effective dramatic points. Choosing an A–BAB structure for his setting, Mozart recapitulates the text of the opening Adagio without slackening from the Allegro that sets in with mention of the sudden reversal of Constanze's fortunes, 'Doch wie schnell schwand meine Freude' ('Yet how quickly my joy vanished'). Mozart recomposed the salient features of the earlier Adagio into the return of the same text in the new tempo, evoking the lost quiet of the opening just as Constanze's thoughts turn back to her happy days with Belmonte.
Dialogue: Constanze sees that the Pasha has been pacing resentfully. She repeats her admiration of him and agrees to be his slave for life, but he must not request a heart promised to another forever. Selim, striving to contain his indignation, interrupts her poignant descrip-

tion of her separation from Belmonte and of her solemn vow of fidelity – she must not provoke his anger even further. She begs for a respite, time to forget her pain. It is a plea he has heard and granted before; he agrees for one last time, one more day. Constanze leaves in despair, breathing the name of her beloved.

Scene 8

Selim finds that her pain, tears and steadfastness only inflame his passion more. Who could use force against such a heart? Pedrillo interrupts his meditations to introduce Belmonte as a young Italian-trained architect. Selim is pleased with him and orders that his needs be seen to for today. Tomorrow he'll discuss with him what he might be able to do. Exit Selim.

Scene 9

The two rejoice, Pedrillo that his plan has worked, Belmonte that he has seen his Constanze. Against his effusions Pedrillo counsels caution. He reminds Belmonte of the sort of land they are in, and suggests they go into the palace garden. But at that moment Osmin appears at the door and blocks their way.

Scene 10

Osmin will hear none of letting Belmonte pass, even though Pedrillo asserts that he has been taken into the Pasha's service. Nor does he care a fig for Belmonte's rank. The Pasha has a soft heart, he declares; he himself has a much better nose for the impostures of such crafty deceivers. Pedrillo declares that they intend to go in, and Osmin again blocks their way.
No. 7 Trio (Osmin, Belmonte, Pedrillo: *Marsch! Marsch! Marsch!*) Osmin threatens them with a beating if they do not leave; they demand that he clear the way; eventually they succeed in driving him from the door and entering the palace grounds.

The practice of omitting the possibly inauthentic four-bar ritornello of this trio, as well as the opening sustained chord of *F* in No. 3, is to be commended. These initial prompts may help an Osmin uncertain of his starting pitch, but they also detract from the impulsive side of his personality Mozart aimed at portraying with his abrupt musical onslaughts in these two numbers.

The rising triadic motive and loose imitative counterpoint of the first act's capstone take up right where Osmin and Belmonte had left off at the end of their magnificent duet earlier (No. 2) – a brilliant musical suggestion of the abiding animosity Osmin is ready to show toward both Belmonte and Pedrillo whenever the least opportunity strikes. Bretzner's text, as Mozart told Leopold on 26 September 1781, suggested the three-voice writing of the opening Allegro section. But the most approved traditions of opera buffa inspired the C major close, Allegro assai (and even faster with the triplet subdivision of the beat), complete with trumpets and drums: 'It must go very fast – and the close should make a good deal of noise – and that's of course everything the end of an act should contain – the more noise, the better; – the shorter, the better – so people don't grow too cool for clapping.'

ACT II

Stage setting: *The garden of Pasha Selim's palace. To one side is Osmin's house.*

Scene 1

Dialogue: Blonde upbraids Osmin for treating her like a common Turkish slave. His quarreling and ordering and grousing are no way to behave toward a European woman.
No. 8 Aria (Blonde: *Durch Zärtlichkeit und Schmeicheln*)
It is easy to win the hearts of good maidens with tenderness, flattery, and complaisance. But grumbling, ordering about, vexing, and blustering will quickly make love as well as fidelity vanish.

With the rondo theme of Blonde's aria Mozart anticipates the opening of his unsurpassed setting of Goethe's 'Das Veilchen' (1785), and in general he strives here for songful simplicity despite the roulades and high tessitura. This is the only number in the opera accompanied by strings alone. Although Bretzner's text consists of a mere two quatrains (and ones of a Metastasian metric cast – three *settenari* and a final *verso tronco*), Mozart spread it over a seven-part rondo pattern. Soon after the première he marked a cut in his autograph which reduced this to five. The rondo, in high fashion at the time, was clearly important to him as a means of expressing in music Blonde's cheerful nature.
Dialogue: Osmin, far from taking the hint Blonde offers him here,

ridicules her for speaking so in Turkey. He is lord, she the slave who must obey him. Blonde laughs. She is an Englishwoman, born to freedom. Osmin, nonplussed by her insolence, orders her to love him. Blonde laughs more heartily and warns him not to come too close to her, if he values his eyes. How can such a hideous old thing dare to order around a young, pretty maid? Turkey doesn't enter into the matter: a woman is a woman wherever she may be, and Turkish women are fools to let themselves be subjugated so. Exasperated, Osmin brings up the subject of Pedrillo, and Blonde freely admits her preference for him. Osmin orders her into the house. She laughs him off. He threatens force, and she reminds him of her position with Constanze, the Pasha's favourite.

Vienna, 1782

Osmin finds himself stymied.

No. 9 Duet (Osmin, Blonde: *Ich gehe, doch rathe ich dir*)

Osmin demands that she avoid Pedrillo; she replies that she is not to be ordered around, even by the Grand Mogul himself. Aside, Osmin wonders how the English can be so foolish as to allow their women such latitude; Blonde reflects that a heart born to liberty will never let itself be treated as a slave, but rather will take pride in its freedom even when it has been lost. Osmin tries a few more commands, which only prompt Blonde to push him away. She readies herself to attack his eyes with her nails if he does not leave. Osmin shrinks timorously from her and departs.

Leipzig, 1781

Osmin realizes that he must dance to the tune she pipes for now. After a final warning about Pedrillo, he goes off angrily as Constanze approaches.

This added duet, a masterpiece of sexual skirmishing, was seemingly added more for Blonde's sake than Osmin's, even though his exit marks the scene's conclusion. She maintains the upper hand throughout, musically as well as tactically. She skilfully counters his heavy-handed commands at the beginning and eventually leads him to the canonic submissiveness of the closing section.

Scene 2

Dialogue: Blonde observes the approach of her mournful mistress. She herself has Pedrillo at least, even if they must meet furtively. Constanze wanders in sadly without seeing Blonde.

Vienna, 1782	*Leipzig, 1781*
No. 10 Recitative and Aria (Constanze: *Welcher Wechsel herrscht in meiner Seele. . . Traurigkeit ward mir zum Loose*) What a change in her soul since the day fate separated her from Belmonte! The joys she knew with him have been replaced by painful longing in her breast.	(The aria only.)

Sorrow has become her fate. Her life now withers like a cankered rose or grass in winter. She may not tell of her soul's bitter pain even to the air; for, unwilling to bear all her complaints, it breathes them back again into her poor heart. (This and Constanze's next aria are discussed in Chapter 5.)

Dialogue: Another day has passed, Constanze laments to Blonde, and still no word from him. And she can scarcely bring herself to think about tomorrow! Blonde does her best to cheer her up. Such a fine evening! One must take heart. Constanze admires Blonde's ability to accept fate so calmly. If only she could do the same!

Vienna, 1782	*Leipzig, 1781*
Blonde says she must keep up hope, but Constanze cannot see a single ray of it. Blonde says she'll never spend her life in despondency, no matter how grim things appear. Constanze counters that flattering oneself with hopes that always prove false brings one nothing but despair. To each her own, shrugs Blonde, but it is still possible that Belmonte could ransom them or else abduct them. They would not be the	Blonde suggests they sing their roundelay: it is a Rondo, and Constanze's favourite piece – so melting, so tender. **Rondeau** (Constanze, Blonde: *Hofnung, Trösterin im Leiden!*) Hope is our comforter in sorrow; it sweetens all our pain. Often, sings Constanze, darkness and the grave frighten the colour from our cheeks. But, replies Blonde, cares and tears vanish at the new day's first

first maids to escape these Turkish gluttons.

glow. When on a stormy night our ship begins to sink, counters Constanze, we are seized with anxiety and see grim death. Then, sings Blonde, a wave bears us in the sleep of death to a mossy bank, and we rest, free from care, in the bosom of sweet hope.

Dialogue: Now, doesn't Constanze feel less oppressed? But just then Blonde catches sight of the Pasha. Constanze does not wish to face him and goes off to find comfort in the lonely shadows.

Blonde spies the Pasha. Constanze does not wish to face him, but he has already spotted them. Blonde leaves, knowing that Selim will send her off anyway if she stays.

Scene 3

Selim reminds her that tomorrow she must love him or else. Must? What a foolish demand! Can love be ordered, like the cut of a new suit of clothes? But here in Turkey anything can be ordered. One must really feel sorry for them; they imprison the objects of their lust and are content simply to gratify their pleasure. Selim asks if she thinks Turkish wives are less happy than those in other lands. Only in that they don't know any better. Constanze affirms that she no longer hopes that her pleas will soften him. She admires him but can never love him. Nor does she fear the power he holds over her, for death is all she has to expect, and the sooner it comes, the better. Not death, rejoins Selim, but tortures of every kind. Those, too, Constanze is ready to bear without fear.

No. 11 Aria (Constanze: *Martern aller Arten*)

Let tortures lie in store for her, she laughs at pain and agony. Only one thing can make her tremble – were she able to be untrue. She begs Selim to be moved and spare her. Heaven's blessing will be his reward. Yet he is determined, she sees. Willingly she chooses pain and affliction. Let him arrange for them, give the order, shout, storm, rave! In the end death will free her. Exit Constanze.

Scene 4

Dialogue: Selim cannot believe he is awake. Where did her courage come from? Perhaps she thinks she will escape. But no, then she would more likely dissemble, so as to put him off his guard. It must be despair! So, with harshness he has got nowhere, nor with pleading. Well, what threats and entreaties cannot do, cunning must effect. Exit Selim.

Scene 5

Blonde returns to find neither Constanze nor Selim. She

pities her mistress, who is too sensitive for the position she is in. Blonde is not sure what she would do in her place, but men are definitely not worth pining to death over. Perhaps she would start thinking like a Muslim.

Blonde pities her mistress heartily.

She catches sight of Pedrillo, who signals secretly to her.

Scene 6

Blonde assures Pedrillo that the coast is clear. He brings news: the end of their slavery is at hand. Belmonte is here, pretending to be an architect; he has a ship ready nearby, and tonight they plan to abduct Constanze and Blonde. At midnight each man will come to his beloved's window with a ladder, after Pedrillo has drugged Osmin with a sleeping potion. Meanwhile, Constanze can meet with Belmonte here in the garden as soon as it is fully dark. Blonde must go report to her.

Vienna, 1782

No. 12 Aria (Blonde: *Welche Wonne, welche Lust*)
What bliss now reigns in her breast. Without delay she will rush to her mistress with the news. With laughter and playfulness she will prophesy joy and jubilation to Constanze's weak, frightened heart. Exit Blonde.

Leipzig, 1781

Exit Blonde.

Scene 7

Dialogue: Pedrillo wishes it were all over, that they were all on the open sea and had seen the last of this cursed land. But it's now or never – he who hesitates is lost.

No. 13 Aria (Pedrillo: *Frisch zum Kampfe*)
Into the fray! Only a coward loses heart. Should he tremble, rather

than boldly wager his life? No – he'll take the chance! Into the fray! Only a coward loses heart.

Mozart mixes here the heroic D major vein he had previously mined in *Idomeneo* with an array of delightful comic touches, mostly thrown out by the orchestra as ironic bystander. That Pedrillo is indeed at base a coward, an essential attribute of the archetype he represents, is ratified by the musical phrase 'Nur ein feiger Tropf verzagt' ('Only a cowardly dolt loses heart'). It crops up again and again, always unchanged, no matter what key or idea has preceded it.

Scene 8

Dialogue: Osmin wonders why Pedrillo sounds so merry. The Pedrillos have never been pessimists, he replies: cheer and wine sweeten the harshest servitude. Too bad the Muslims can't understand that, poor devils. Yes, Muhammad really muffed it badly when he banned wine. Pedrillo shows the suspicious Osmin two bottles of Cypriot wine, seats himself Turkish-style, and drinks from the smaller one. Osmin bids him drink from the larger bottle as well. Pedrillo chides him for thinking he would try to poison him and takes a sip from the big bottle. Hesitantly, Osmin accepts it from Pedrillo, who assures him that Muhammad is doubtless long asleep by now, and has better things to worry about than a bottle of wine.
No. 14 Duet (Pedrillo, Osmin: *Vivat, Bachus!*)
Pedrillo praises Bacchus – he was a clever fellow! Osmin is still unsure about daring to drink the wine: could Allah be watching? Pedrillo encourages him, and Osmin finally gulps it down. They join in praising women – blondes, brunettes, long live all of them! The wine tastes splendid, true ambrosia! They both praise Bacchus, who invented it.

Bretzner had intended Osmin's inebriation to begin in the dialogue succeeding this duet, but Mozart could not resist working the early effects of the drugged wine into the music itself, with the main tune compressed from four to three bars toward the end.
Dialogue: Pedrillo declares there is nothing to equal wine – not even women and money. It banishes all vexation, it never frowns at him the way his sweetheart does sometimes. Osmin, who begins to feel the effects of the sleeping potion, agrees it is a fine thing, it makes one so cheerful, so contented. Does he have any more? Pedrillo gives him the rest of the small bottle. Osmin begins to waver about, and his

speech becomes more and more slurred as he entreats Pedrillo not to betray him to the Pasha. Pedrillo convinces him to go off to bed before the Pasha discovers them. He helps Osmin into his house, then returns at once.

Scene 9

Pedrillo imitates the drugged Osmin. That was easy work, but it is still three hours to midnight, and he could easily sleep it off in that time. Belmonte appears, looking for Constanze. She comes along a path and Belmonte rushes to embrace her. During this and the ensuing conversation of the lovers, Pedrillo pantomimes to Blonde the episode with Osmin, and also how he will come to her window at midnight with a ladder in order to abduct her. Meanwhile Belmonte and Constanze give voice to their rapture at being in one another's arms again after so many days of anxiety and sorrow. Constanze, weeping at her beloved's breast, realizes that joy, too, has its tears.

Vienna, 1782

[The episode in the column to the right is omitted here and used instead as the core of the quartet (No. 16) at the end of Act II. In its place appears the following, manufactured from the first sentence of the omitted dialogue:]

No. 15 Aria (Belmonte: *Wenn der Freude Thränen fliessen*)

When tears of joy flow, love is smiling on the loved one. For him to kiss them from her cheek is love's sweetest and greatest reward. To see Constanze full of rapture, to press her to his heart, is worth more than all the riches of Croesus. To think of never seeing each other again! Yet now they need not feel the pain separation can bring.

Leipzig, 1781

Belmonte would like to kiss them away and hopes they will be the last. But then he asks her if it is true that she is the Pasha's lover. She protests: could he really believe her untrue? She paints a picture of her days: sleepless nights, sighs, and prayers to heaven for his protection. Belmonte entreats her forgiveness for his mistrust. He renews his eternal pledge with a kiss.

This and the next aria for Adamberger at the beginning of Act III seem to have cost Mozart considerable trouble. In the present case excisions and alterations both in the autograph and in early printed and manuscript sources serve both to reduce the aria's dimensions (from seven parts to five, as in the case of Blonde's rondo in Act II) and also to ease its considerable demands on the tenor.

Dialogue: To business: he has a ship ready, and when everyone is asleep at midnight he will appear at Constanze's window, and then may love be their guardian angel! Pedrillo tells Blonde that when he sings something in the street, as is his custom, she must be on the alert. He who has everything to lose must venture all.

Vienna, 1782

Belmonte and Constanze determine to put their trust in love and to hope for the best.

No. 16 Quartet (Constanze, Belmonte, Pedrillo, Blonde: *Ach Belmonte! ach mein Leben!*)

Constanze and Belmonte repeat their raptures, tears and kisses from earlier in the scene. Pedrillo also repeats his clarification of the escape plans with Blonde. Now hope's sun shines on them through a turbid firmament. The end of their sorrow is in sight. Belmonte expresses misgivings, however, over rumours that she loves the Pasha, which reduces her to tears. Pedrillo, too, wonders if Blonde is worth so much danger, since Osmin may have exercised his rights as her master. Blonde boxes his ears, which enlightens him at once. Belmonte, too, sees the error of his ways and kneels to beg Constanze's pardon. The ladies relate the base accusations of their lovers to each other. The

Leipzig, 1781

Quartet (Belmonte, Constanze, Blonde, Pedrillo: *Mit Pauken und Trompeten*)

Pedrillo: Heroes enter the lists with trumpets and drums, boldness and strength, and they carry the day. Blonde: A hero's courage enlivens even the heart of a weak maiden. Despite trepidation, anxiety and quaking, victory is her reward in the end. Belmonte: for his beloved should he not dare all? Even to bear chains for her would be a sweet reward. Constanze: what does she care for dangers? Only in him does she find joy. To suffer death for him would be a sweet reward to her. All four: how their hearts beat for joy! They will hasten away through sea and flood on the wings of love.

men, convinced of their loyalty, renew their pleas for forgiveness. Blonde will have none of it, and Constanze cannot yet recover from her disbelief. But at length the men's remorse wins their pardon and, the dispute settled, all four join in praise of love and the hope that nothing will kindle jealousy's flame again.

Although the dramatic pretext for this quartet is slight, Mozart's overall musical architecture demanded such a keystone here at the end of Act II. The dynamic straining at the leash in the confrontational duets, Nos. 2 and 9, finds here its lone opportunity for fulfilment.

Mozart calls this number simply 'Quartetto', but in fact it draws almost exclusively on Italian finale practices for its musical resources. Stephanie had marked off the major sections of the little drama in the manner of the Italians, with changes in poetic metre (trochaic, iambic, trochaic again, and – for the last four lines – dactylic). Mozart's plan of keys and tempos follows this scheme up to a point, but he reserves the return of the tonic for the end of the second trochaic section, where the ladies at last dispense forgiveness for the unfounded suspicions of the men.

One could dwell on every detail of this great ensemble. Let us take but one example, the celebrated Andantino passage, 'Wenn unsrer Ehre wegen' (bars 193–208). In itself a beautiful homophonic rumination in siciliano tempo, its transcendent effect derives from the place it occupies in the finale's music-dramatic curve. The workings of Belmonte's and Pedrillo's jealousy have brought the protagonists to a moment akin in its own modest way to the sublime crux of *Le nozze di Figaro*, when the Count kneels to beg the Countess's forgiveness. The reflections of the four in Stephanie's verses do not in themselves merit Mozart's expansive, quasi-choral vestments, but the turning-point in the lovers' falling out does.

ACT III

Stage setting: *A plaza in front of the Pasha's palace. To one side is the palace itself, and across from it is Osmin's house. In the background a view of the sea. It is midnight.*

Scene 1

Dialogue: Pedrillo appears with the sailor Klaas, who carries a ladder. [In the original libretto (Leipzig, 1781) Klaas speaks his few lines in Lower Saxon dialect.] Pedrillo has him put down the ladder and return to the ship to fetch a second one. His heart is beating furiously, especially since these Turks aren't to be trifled with. Klaas brings the second ladder, and Pedrillo tells him to weigh anchor, set sail, and await his cargo. Exit Klaas.

Scene 2

Pedrillo's heart and breathing betray his intense anxiety. Belmonte appears. Pedrillo tells him to sing something, which he himself does each evening. Every hour a night watch of Janissaries make their rounds here, and they are used to hearing his singing. Pedrillo leaves to scout about the palace.

Scene 3

Belmonte's heart, too, beats wildly. The closer the moment comes, the more his anxious soul grows faint. May love be his guide!

No. 17 Aria (Belmonte: *Ich baue ganz auf deine Stärke*) He puts all his hope and trust in the power of love, for what wonders has it not often brought to pass! What appears impossible to all the world still finds fulfilment through love.

Quintet with Chorus (Belmonte, Pedrillo, Constanze, Osmin, a mute, Blonde, the watch: *Welch ängstliches Beben* = Scenes 3–5) Accompanying himself on the mandolin, Belmonte sings of the anxious trembling and longing in his blood. As if in a storm, he is tossed between fear and hope. Who can give him peace and assuage his pain?

Scene 4

Dialogue: Pedrillo returns and says everyone is asleep. Belmonte is anxious to get going, but Pedrillo must first give the signal. He sends Belmonte off to stand guard at the corner, then picks up the mandolin.

[Quintet continues:] Pedrillo says everyone is asleep. Belmonte is anxious to get going, but Pedrillo must first sing his little song. When he coughs during it, he will pick up the ladder and they will be inside in no time. He sends Belmonte to stand guard in a rosemary bush. Pedrillo hopes for a quick escape, otherwise a strangling is inevitable. He hears a noise and panics, but Belmonte tells him it was only the wind.

No. 18 Romanze (Pedrillo: *In Mohrenland gefangen war*)
A lovely maid was held captive in the land of the Moors. She sighed and wept day and night for her release. A young knight came from abroad, took pity on her, and pledged his head and his honour to rescue her.

Dialogue: All appears to be well. Belmonte urges him to finish, but Pedrillo claims it is no fault of his that the ladies haven't appeared. He sends Belmonte back to his post and continues his song:

Pedrillo pauses: all is well. Belmonte urges him to finish, Pedrillo warns him to stay on guard.

Romanze [conclusion]: 'I'll come to you in the dark of night,' cried the knight. 'Let me in quickly. I fear neither castle nor guards: at midnight you shall be free.' And so it was: at midnight, there he was, and she gave him her tender hand. Early the next day the empty cell was found – they were gone.

This is the only operatic Romanze Mozart ever wrote, yet he captured immediately all the complex music–dramatic potential with which this deceptively simple Franco-German genre had been invested. This tradition and Mozart's beguiling and apposite specimen of the narrative Romanze are treated in Chapter 5.

Dialogue: Pedrillo coughs several times, and Constanze opens her window. Pedrillo sets one ladder there, and Belmonte climbs up and enters. Now, observes Pedrillo, things are in earnest: it's life or death, and he shudders to think of the methods they will use if he is caught. Belmonte and Constanze come out of the door. He rejoices, but she is so afraid she

Quintet continues: (Virtually the same, but in verse and more succinct.)

can scarcely stand up. Pedrillo whisks them both off. He puts the second ladder under Blonde's window, bids Cupid steady it for him, and clambers up. He calls for her to open, she does, and in he goes.

Scene 5

Osmin, still half asleep, appears at his door with a black mute, who gesticulates that something is amiss. Osmin sends him to investigate; he finds the ladder and indicates it to his master. Osmin is certain that thieves and murderers have broken into his house. He sends the mute for the watch. He himself stands guard at the ladder, but soon nods off. Pedrillo gingerly begins descending the ladder, but Blonde spots Osmin. He awakens and catches sight of Pedrillo as he re-enters the window; Osmin sends up a cry of 'Thief!' and climbs after him. Pedrillo and Blonde slip out of the front door and steal away. Osmin comes after them but is detained by the watch, who mistake him for the malefactor. Osmin claims that he is the overseer of the Pasha's gardens.

Twice the guards try to lead Osmin off, but he resists. The mute returns and tries to explain with gesticulation who Osmin really is. A part of the watch returns with Pedrillo and Blonde.

A part of the watch returns with Pedrillo and Blonde. Osmin wants Pedrillo's head

[This section absent.]

taken off at once. Pedrillo claims he had only taken Blonde for a walk, since (he whispers to him) Osmin himself was incapacitated earlier owing to the wine. But Osmin will hear none of it.

Another part of the watch brings in Belmonte and Constanze. Osmin sees himself vindicated in his mistrust of them. Belmonte tries to bribe him with a bag of money, but it is his head, not his gold that Osmin craves. He will hear no further pleas from them; he orders the watch to drag all four off to the Pasha. Exeunt all but Osmin.

(Virtually the same, but in verse and more succinct.)

Exeunt all.

No. 19 Aria (Osmin: *O! wie will ich triumphiren*)

Osmin exults in the prospect of their all being hanged as he laughs and jumps and sings for joy. 'You damned harem-mice come slinking around, but our ear has heard you, and we have caught you in our nets before you could escape!' Exit Osmin.

(The first line is drawn from one of Osmin's exclamations near the end of the above ensemble.)

As has frequently been noticed, the main tune of Osmin's Rondo resembles the first theme of the equally unbridled Presto finale of the Haffner Symphony (K.385, completed just as the *Entführung* was going into production). The aria is Fischer's triumph as well as Osmin's, exploring every aspect of his voice's range and agility.

Transformation

Stage setting: *The chamber of the Pasha.*

Scene 6

Dialogue: Selim, awakened by the din, learns from Osmin of the attempted abduction and the foiling of it, for which (says Osmin) he has his faithful servant's vigilance to thank. The watch bring in Belmonte and Constanze, and Selim upbraids them both for their abuse of his forbearance and kindness. Constanze admits her guilt, but everything she did was for her sole love, for whose life she will now gladly render up her own. Belmonte goes down on his knees before the Pasha to plead for compassion.

Vienna, 1782

He is from a great Spanish family, the Lostados; the Pasha can demand what ransom fee he pleases. The name stuns Selim. He quickly ascertains that Belmonte is the son of his greatest enemy, the Commandant of Oran, whose greed tore Selim's beloved from his arms and deprived him of honour and fortune as well. Because of him Selim was forced to flee his homeland. He determines to deal with Belmonte as his father had dealt with him. Selim leaves with Osmin in order to prepare their torture.

Leipzig, 1781

Each of the two tries to convince the Pasha that the other should be held guiltless and he or she alone be allowed to die. Selim terminates their entreaties with the promise that they shall both die. Constanze is rapturous over the prospect of dying in Belmonte's arms.

Scene 7

No. 20 Recitative and Duet (Belmonte, Constanze: *Welch ein Geschick! o Qual der Seele! . . . Meinetwegen sollst du sterben!*)

What agony of the soul! Because of Belmonte, Constanze is undone! She tells him not to torment himself. Death is but a pathway to peace. [Omitted from the first edition: Her angelic soul brings comfort to his shaken heart and softens the pain of death. And yet, he is

Duet (Belmonte, Constanze: *Ach, von deinem Arm umschlungen*)

In each others' arms they welcome the angel of death. They shall sink smiling into their graves. What bliss to be united in Elysium, to be on a peaceful shore in that unknown land.

drawing her to her grave!]
[Duet]: Because of him she must die! Constanze turns this about: he dies because of her – she drew him to destruction. To die with him is bliss. Their sole wish had been to live together; without the other, to remain yet living is nothing but pain. Gladly and in peace each will die for the other. What a blessing! To die with one's beloved is holy rapture. With joyous glances one leaves the world.

Mozart's high musical ambitions in the *Entführung* reach their zenith in this great recitative and duet. Stephanie's text replaces a dramatically static one by Bretzner which begins after the lovers have determined to meet death together. In contrast, Stephanie's allows Mozart to explore the transformation of Belmonte's anguish and self-reproach through the balm of Constanze's quiet courage. The recitative, which was possibly added at the last minute, is a masterly portrayal of these hitherto unexplored emotions – Belmonte's with the opening swells, caught between F major and D minor, and Constanze's with ethereal accents in E♭ major, a key of consolation he comes to accept later in the recitative, and which also figures importantly in the duet.

So deeply expressive is Mozart's music here that one is tempted to think of his own situation in mid-1782, when it was most probably composed – alone in Vienna and betrothed to Constanze Weber against his father's wishes. Could it have been more than the drama itself that inspired him to empty the stage here so that Belmonte and Constanze sing this sublime music not for the benefit of the Pasha, as they do in Bretzner's version, but for each other alone?

Dialogue: The Pasha is almost moved by their steadfastness. Osmin, however, is affronted by such temerity. His anger is quickly redirected by the arrival of another part of the guard with Pedrillo and Blonde. Pedrillo confesses, pleading his love for

Scene 8

Another part of the guard brings in Pedrillo and Blonde. All is lost, he tells Belmonte and Constanze. He has heard that they are to be soaked in oil and then impaled. Blonde, since she must die, declares herself indifferent to the method used. Pedrillo cannot share in her resoluteness.

Last Scene

The Pasha, his entourage and a joyous Osmin return. Belmonte is prepared to hear the Pasha's judgment, to atone for his father's sins, and to blame Selim for nothing. Selim observes that taking revenge for granted must be why Belmonte's race perpetrates so many injustices. But Selim has despised his father too much to follow in his footsteps. 'Take your freedom, take Constanze, sail to your homeland, say to your father that you were in my power, that I freed you so that you could say to him: it was a far greater pleasure to requite a suffered injustice with good deeds than to repay vice with vice.' If Belmonte will grow to be more human that his father, then Selim's actions are rewarded. Constanze attempts to express her admiration, but Selim stops her; he hopes she will never regret having refused his heart.

Pedrillo asks for mercy, but Osmin claims he has deserved death a hundred times over. 'Let him seek it in his

his fiancée Blonde, homesickness, and Osmin's tormenting of her. Selim cuts him off and orders them all strangled at once. As some of the Turks approach the four with silk ropes, the lovers utter their final words. Selim hears Constanze speak Belmonte's name. A quick series of inquiries convinces him that Belmonte is his own son, left in the monastery of St Sebastian when only four years old. He asks to embrace the son he has sought so long in vain. Both Belmonte and Constanze fall to their knees. He bids them both stand up and be his children.

Aria (Constanze: *Ah, mit freudigem Entzücken*)

With joyous ecstasy her ardent song flows, and the rapturous thanks of her heart mount to the sky. Already she was surrounded by fears of death and believed herself already departed; her spirit floated in a higher realm. (Da capo.)

Pedrillo and Blonde also dare to ask for Selim's pardon, which he grants over Osmin's objection that Pedrillo has

homeland, then,' replies Selim, and, handing Belmonte a passport, he instructs that all four be conducted to their ship. Osmin cannot believe that his Blonde is to go as well, but the Pasha asks whether Osmin values his eyes: 'I am providing for you better than you think.' What one cannot win over with good deeds one must do without.

No. 21a Vaudeville (Belmonte, Constanze, Pedrillo, Blonde, Osmin: *Nie werd' ich deine Huld verkennen*)
Each of the lovers expresses his gratitude to Selim, and all join in the sentiment that anyone who can forget such kindness is to be despised. Belmonte will always and everywhere proclaim him great and noble. Constanze will not forget what she owes him, even in the delight of love. Pedrillo will not soon forget, either, how close to a strangling he came. Blonde thanks the Pasha for the accommodations, but confesses she is glad to be leaving. 'For just look at that animal!' she remarks, pointing to Osmin. 'Can anyone bear such a thing?' Osmin bursts in that these deceiving dogs should be burnt. His tongue fairly bristles in his mouth to pronounce their fate. He repeats his litany of tortures from Act I deserved death a hundred times over.

Ready to burst with exasperation, Osmin asks that at least Pedrillo be made to give him his slave Blonde, but Selim says she is Pedrillo's. As a token of friendship Pedrillo offers Osmin his hand, but Osmin would as soon shake hands with the devil and stomps off.

(No. 3): 'First beheaded, then hanged, then impaled on heated poles, then tied up and drowned, and finally flayed.' Exit Osmin.

Nothing is so hateful as revenge, the others observe, but to be humane, kind, and to forgive unselfishly are things only great souls can do. He who cannot recognise this is to be despised.

No. 21b Chorus of Janissaries (Chorus: *Bassa Selim lebe lange*)

'Long live Pasha Selim! May honour be his property, may his gracious head be decked with jubilation and renown.'

Amid general rejoicing, Blonde reminds Constanze that she had always told her that hope never leads to disgrace:

Chorus (Constanze, Blonde, Belmonte, Pedrillo: *Oft wölkt stürmisch sich der Himmel*)

Often the sky fills with storm clouds, and we see with terror night and horrifying turmoil. But a ray of gentle sunlight quickly turns distress to rapture and joy.

5 *The musical language of the opera*

'Turkish' music in Oriental opera

In Mozart's first letter to Leopold about Bretzner's libretto he remarked, 'I am going to compose the sinfonia, the chorus in the first act, and the closing chorus with Turkish music' (1 August 1781). By 'Turkish music' Mozart referred to an opaque, Westernised derivative based loosely on what little was known of actual Turkish music – a cultural distortion not so different from that of the Turkish personages that this music accompanied on European stages.[1]

What music of the Turks the West knew at first hand consisted almost solely of the military music of the Janissary band, or *mehter*. In battle these musicians grouped themselves around the standard and played continuously throughout an encounter, instilling courage in the Turkish soldiers and fear in their foe with the racket they raised. Western witnesses were impressed. C. F. D. Schubart described its vigorous character: 'No other genre of music requires such a firm, decided, and overpoweringly predominant beat. The first beat of each measure is so strongly marked with a new and manly accent that it is virtually impossible to get out of step.'[2]

During the eighteenth century it became fashionable for European armies to import corps of Turkish musicians along with their instruments and attire. Western composers, however, were far less willing to proceed so literally in their operas, ballets, and instrumental works intended to evoke a Turkish ambiance. Instead they approximated. For example, Janissary music was monophonic and rhythmically complex in its patterning. European composers, in their own versions, created by analogy a spare harmonic texture and used duple metre with firm downbeats and repetitive rhythmic patterns. A specific instrumental group, the so-called *batterie turque*, mimicked the sounds of an actual Janissary band with cymbals, triangle, tambourine and bass drum. The triangle in fact is never mentioned as a Turkish instrument and appears only in these Western imitations.

Along with this, composers developed a thesaurus of motivic elements belonging to the *stilo alla turca*. As Miriam Whaples points out, 'The two Janissary choruses of the *Entführung aus dem Serail* are a compendium of "Turkish" mannerisms, there being scarcely a detail of the style that is not found in one or the other of the choruses.'[3] From her discussion we can extract seven 'Turkish' elements which the *Entführung* holds in common with other Oriental operas of its day (they apply equally to Mozart's earlier non-operatic essays in this style, particularly the finales of the A major violin concerto K.219, and piano sonata K.331):

1 *Repeated thirds in the melody, sometimes alternating with fifths.* This feature saw extremely widespread use in the cadential formula Mozart employed in the opera's closing chorus (Ex. 2). Bence Szabolcsi has remarked on its appearance in Hungarian folk melodies called *törökös* (*à la turque*).[4]

Ex. 2

2 *Escaped notes or upper thirds decorating a descending scale.* Mozart favoured this figure in both Janissary choruses, as seen in Ex. 3*a* and *b*.

Ex. 3*a*

3 *Repeated notes in both the melody and especially the accompaniment.* Often they are decorated by short grace notes. Gluck underscored the vigour of this device with horns and cymbals in the overture to *La Rencontre imprévue* (Ex. 4).

Ex. 4

4 *2/4 metre.* Evident in nearly all of the examples we have cited.
5 *Long initial note values followed by quicker ones.* Again, both of Mozart's choruses and Gluck's overture offer clear examples.
6 *Preference for harmonic relations of a third.* One thinks of the interplay of A minor and C major at the beginning of the first Janissary chorus in the *Entführung* (Ex. 5), reinforced in the middle section for four soloists (A – F – A).[5]

Ex. 5

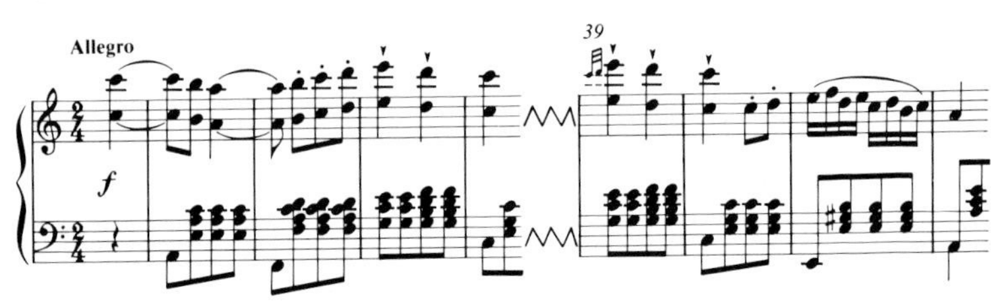

7 *Modal scalar inflections, most often a raised fourth.* Whaples claims that the prominent raised fourth in Ex. 6*a* does not appear in other 'Turkish' pieces, but Gluck had used it in the monophonic gibberish air of the Calender in *La Rencontre imprévue*, 'Castagno, castagna', as well as in the opera's overture (Ex. 6*b* and *c*). Such passing appeals to the Lydian mode were obviously evocations of the exotic in an age so exclusively devoted to the major–minor system.

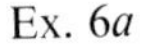
Ex. 6*a*

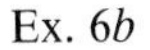

Ex. 6*b*

Ex. 6*c*

Earlier Oriental operas had turned to the *stilo alla turca* mostly for instrumental numbers (such as overtures and marches) and for choruses. Mozart, too, provided for the style in these categories, but he also saw fit to work it in elsewhere in the opera. Certainly, he was aware of the partiality of the Viennese for this style. As Friedrich Nicolai noticed on visiting the city in 1781, 'Turkish' music could be heard in the Prater as a part of the rich Viennese tradition of open-air music.[6] In his letter to Leopold of 26 September 1781, Mozart stresses the close connexion of several of his 'Turkish' numbers and current Viennese taste. 'The Janissary chorus [in Act I] is everything one could wish a Janissary chorus to be,' he wrote, 'short and jolly; – and written completely for the Viennese.' He also mentions 'the drinking duet (for the Messrs. Viennese) ['das Saufduett ‖ : per li Sig:ri vieneri : ‖'] which consists of nothing other than my Turkish tattoo'. The duet in question, 'Vivat, Bachus', in fact became the immediate delight of Viennese audiences and their favourite number in the opera.

Mozart was not simply pandering to popular taste with these *alla turca* items. Rather, they play a part in an overall strategy, one that envisaged a definite dramatic role for elements of the 'Turkish' style throughout the opera. The most significant consequence of this strategy was something that set Mozart's opera apart from all earlier Oriental operas – the integration of the 'Turkish' style into the general musical language of the opera.

Integration of the 'Turkish' style: Osmin

As a dramatic rather than merely colouristic device, Mozart's 'Turkish' music functions most clearly in scenes of conflict and contrast. Not surprisingly, nearly all of these involve his greatest musical portrait in the opera – that of Osmin. No other character has so deeply interested critics, who unite in proclaiming him completely Mozart's creation. Fascination with Osmin has in fact been a source of a great deal of misunderstanding surrounding the opera itself. Ignoring Bretzner's description of him as 'overseer of the Pasha's country estate' with his own house across the street from the palace, many writers have assumed that Osmin is the keeper of Selim's harem. Saint-Foix went so far as to call him a eunuch, 'exempt, par nature, de toute tentation', and as early as 1818 Ludwig Börne tried to make psychological hay with the same erroneous assumption:

> Such a masterful fellow, such a transfigured grumbler and fawning guardian of wives, who torments himself in fury at the locked grating, through which he daily sees the honey which he may not lick, such an angry fellow, who hates all the world, because he *cannot* love, will not soon be set to music again.[7]

These and other writers were certainly not moved to their fascination with Osmin because of his dramatic role in the plot, which is a minor one. Bretzner had thought principally in terms of a skilled actor: his Osmin sings only four times and only one of these times alone (in his strophic song 'Wer ein Liebchen hat gefunden'). In Stephanie's version, by contrast, Osmin sings in seven of his eight scenes, including two new arias and two new duets. Of all the characters in the opera, he gains most significantly in musical numbers from one version to the other.

Mozart, we know, prompted every one of Stephanie's additions for Osmin. But how much had he been thinking in terms of Osmin himself and how much in terms of the bass Ludwig Fischer? (Recall his remark to Leopold on 26 September 1781: 'Such a man has to be made use of, especially since he has the public here wholly on his side.') By good fortune Mozart could think of both. Since lack of moderation and self-control lay at the heart of the Turkish type Osmin represents, no harm would come to the drama if he injected his personality as often as he pleased, nor would this hurt Mozart's stock with the fickle Viennese public he hoped to win over.

Mozart's letter of 26 September goes on from his comment about Fischer to a discussion of Osmin's first aria, 'Solche hergelauf'ne

Laffen' – a passage which has probably been quoted more often than anything else Mozart ever wrote, for it seeks to explain and defend aesthetically the aria's unusual coda:

But this Osmin has just the one little song to sing in the original libretto, and otherwise nothing except for the trio [ending Act I] and finale [i.e. the Act III elopement scene]. Therefore he has been given an aria in the first act and will have yet another in the second. – I've given the whole aria to Herr Stephanie; – and the main portion of the music for it was finished before Stephanie knew a word about it. – You have only the beginning of it and the end, which must be of good effect – Osmin's anger is made comic by having Turkish music introduced there. – In working out the aria I've let his [Fischer's] beautiful deep tones gleam forth. – The '*Drum beym Barte des Propheten*' etc. is in the same tempo, to be sure, but with fast notes – and as his anger continues to grow, then – just when the aria seems to be over – the Allegro assai in a completely different measure and in another key must create the finest effect; for a man in such a towering rage oversteps all order, measure, and limit, he does not know himself – so the music, too, must no longer know itself – but since the passions, be they powerful or not, must never be expressed to the point of disgust, and music, even in the most horrifying situation, must never offend the ear, but must actually please, and consequently remain music, thus I've not chosen a key foreign to F (the key of the aria) but a key allied to it, yet not the closest, D minor, but rather the more distant one of A minor.

Mozart articulates four clear compositional guidelines which he followed in setting the aria: (1) The situation rather than the specific text generated the essential musical material. Mozart claims to have created the aria's main ideas even before a text for them had been written. (2) Fischer's skills were to be shown to greatest advantage. (3) The ruling passion – boiling rage – should shape the aria's formal plan, but even in depicting such an immoderate and uncontrollable emotion the composer must not abandon moderation and control. (4) 'Turkish' music was to be introduced not to heighten the brutal sadism possessing Osmin at the end but rather to render his unbridled anger comical.

So artfully did Mozart blend traitional 'Turkish' features and general musical tokens of rage that it is difficult to separate them: the monophonic opening with progressively shorter note values, the heavily accented cut time, menacing half-steps, irregular phrase lengths, diminished seventh chords, obsessive repetition of figures rising by step, upward-mounting scalar thrusts, incisive dynamic contrast and frequent *f–p* punctuation.

Fischer's voice evoked specific traits which we can identify from other arias which composers at Vienna wrote for him. Salieri, for example, had included in the first aria of Herr Bär in *Der Rauchfangkehrer* the same low sustained notes and rapid repeated figures familiar in 'Solche hergelauf'ne Laffen' (Ex. 7). Rapid rising scales from the depths capitalise on one of Fischer's great assets in Gebler's estimation, his ability to 'sing the deepest tones with a fullness, agility, and grace otherwise found only among good tenors'.[8]

Ex. 7

Mozart concentrates chiefly on explaining to Leopold the aria's unusual double coda and particularly the close in A minor. In the first coda the pace already quickens, he notes, as Osmin fixates more and more obsessively on single motives, rhythms and pitches. Dynamic contrast grows manic, the harmonies compulsively cadential. The surprising second coda – coming after dialogue in a new tempo, metre and key, and with 'Turkish' instrumentation – does 'create the finest effect', as Mozart wished. Nor is the key really so distant. By sliding down from F at the end of the first coda to the E beginning the second, Osmin echoes the important half-step which had opened the aria. Its sinister implication of A minor (which the monophonic texture had done nothing to contradict) now comes out into the open, as does the hint of obsessive reiteration of *F–E* suggested by the opening measures (Ex. 8). Osmin will come back to this same half-step pivot between F major and A minor in the Vaudeville at the end of the opera.

Ex. 8

Mozart's unexpected and tonally eccentric coda, thanks to the famous passage he wrote to Leopold defending its dramatic role, has achieved the status of a celebrated solecism. Yet it represents only one – and by no means the boldest – such stylistic divagation in the *Entführung*. The tonal ambiguity of Pedrillo's Romanze in Act III offers another instance, and the very overture breaks one of the fundamental laws of Viennese Classicism by failing to recapitulate its dominant-based secondary material in the tonic during the reprise.

By far the most striking formal eccentricity appears in No. 2, the splendid Lied and duet of Osmin and Belmonte. Here the tonal irregularity Mozart had broached in composing 'Solche hergelauf'ne Laffen' permeates the entire dramatic conception of the interchange between Belmonte and Osmin:

Andante	Allegro				Presto
Lied	Duet				
g	B♭ E♭ F	–a	C/c g	E♭ B♭	D

Here, too, Mozart reveals the full arsenal on which he will draw in the opera's later scenes of confrontation. The opening Lied is conceived in the style of a 6/8 Romanze (later heard as well in Pedrillo's serenade 'In Mohrenland'). André had turned his back on Bretzner's dramatic aims by setting Osmin's song as an unvaried strophic Lied in G major, ignoring the interaction between Belmonte and Osmin which already begins here (see Synopsis). It did not escape Mozart, on the other hand, that the surly, suspicious overseer aims his second and third stanzas directly at the unwelcome stranger. In each one the orchestral accompaniment grows more agitated and harmonically charged,[9] and Osmin's animosity even erupts into a brief Allegro outburst ('oft lauscht da ein junges Herrchen') in the third stanza, the first of many to come.

The duet itself divides into two main sections. The first, a series of increasingly heated exchanges, moves freely around a constellation of keys related to B♭ major. From a low energy level of antiphonal questions and mimicking answers in E♭ and F, the temperature begins to rise in earnest when Belmonte mentions Pedrillo to Osmin. An aside for both in A minor introduces imitative counterpoint, a tool Mozart uses again and again to heighten the hostile atmosphere Osmin never fails to create throughout the opera. Belmonte tries a new tack in C major, to be answered promptly with Osmin's mimicry in C minor. More imitative counterpoint leads to one of Fischer's strong suits – rapid conjunct passages in rising quavers. It comes to a head with the same cadence figure that closes the second coda of 'Solche hergelaufne Laffen' – a neat parallel, for in both places Osmin is giving free rein to the same sadistic sentiments (Ex. 9*a* and *b*).

Ex. 9*a*

Ex. 9*b*

Thereafter Belmonte tries to return to his opening gambit in E♭. This time Osmin does not let him so much as finish his sentence but injects his own sarcastic interpretation of his intentions. By augmented sixth, B♭ major yields to the dominant of D minor and the duet accelerates into its concluding section.

Everything Mozart said about the A minor coda of Osmin's aria applies to the Presto, which concludes the duet in a new key, a new metre and a new tempo. Mozart carries on the contrapuntal interplay of the foregoing with a loose canon set to fugue-like entries. The rising triadic thirds of 'Scheert euch zum Teufel!' will return in Osmin's further musical confrontations with the Europeans – in the trio ending Act I ('Marsch, marsch, marsch!') and in his Act II duet with Blonde (with 'O Engländer, seid ihr nicht Toren'). The motif could be interpreted as a 'Turkish' feature, for it is part and parcel of Mozart's 'Turkish' manner, as both the overture and the first Janissary chorus illustrate. But, like other ingredients of this style, it has been absorbed here into the opera's life-blood.

But it was not solely the character of Osmin that inspired Mozart to think of how the role of 'Turkish' music in the opera might be expanded beyond a purely colouristic one. For even in the most traditional context of all for this style – the two Janissary choruses – Mozart moved beyond the purely decorative. He appears to have been the only composer of his time to have abandoned verisimilitude by writing his 'Janissary' choruses for female as well as male voices. Perhaps his decision was partly timbral, but it also makes an important dramatic point. For the presence of the women (whom the stage director is left free to interpret as slaves, wives, or both) works a transformation on the traditional 'Turkish' values associated with Eastern males – force and sexual prowess. Through the addition of the women's voices Mozart suggests a more universal celebration of the generosity, largeness of mind and clemency displayed by the Pasha. In this sense Selim, though he does not sing, does have his own music.

Architecture: dialogue, music and tonal plan

Mozart's integral approach to his musical portrayal of Osmin and his enlarged sense of music's role in the opera as a whole had to make their peace not only with a libretto written for another composer working in another tradition, but also with the inherent limitations which comic opera in German imposed on him. Most obvious of all was its use of spoken dialogue rather than the simple recitative of the Italians. This preference, shared with French comic opera, was not simply a linguistic one, but rather sprang from the strong historical roots of both genres in spoken comedy.

To a thoughtful composer, the presence of spoken dialogue posed several problems. Musical numbers in a dialogue-rich libretto could easily sound like lyric byways, modestly enhancing already well-developed characters and situations, or worse, serving up gratuitous or platitudinous aphorisms. Even under the best of circumstances there remained the very palpable aesthetic jolt created each time the piece shifted from spoken word to musical utterance.

In the *Entführung* Mozart makes use of several strategies which suggest his own sensitivity to this issue. He had Stephanie turn Belmonte's opening monologue into the song 'Hier soll ich dich denn sehen', minimising the role of the spoken word until after the drama has weighed anchor with the Lied and duet of Osmin and Belmonte. Only a few lines of speech intervene between the two numbers, and Mozart begins the Lied's brief ritornello already in mid-sentence, so to speak, on a i_6 chord in the middle of a bar (Ex. 10). As a result, the

Ex. 10

opening scene – composed of arietta, Lied and duet – begins to approximate to what Mozart will later call an Introduzione in *Don Giovanni.*

Mozart avails himself of other devices to bridge the gap between spoken word and song. He begins some numbers off-centre tonally or syntactically, creating the effect of taking up the music already in progress. On other occasions he mediates with the most traditional form of sung speech – recitative.

A technique Mozart had used with impressive effect in *Zaïde* – melodrama – does not appear in the *Entführung*. In 1778 Mozart had written to his father full of enthusiasm for this new genre after hearing Georg Benda's *Medea* at Mannheim:

In truth, nothing has ever surprised me so much! – for I had always imagined such a thing would have no effect! – You of course know that in it there is no singing, only declamation – and the music is like an obbligato recitative – occasionally there is speech along with the music, which then makes the most splendid effect. . . You know what my opinion would be? – Most recitatives in opera ought to be treated in this manner – and only occasionally, when the words *can be expressed well in music* should there be singing in recitative (12 November 1778).

As Mozart implies here, melodrama offered an alternative to obbligato recitative, not spoken dialogue: it best served intensely wrought moments involving serious personages, such as Gomatz and Soliman in *Zaïde.* Somehow Belmonte and Constanze did not offer plausible opportunities for its use in the *Entführung.* Pasha Selim, on the other hand, presented a very attractive possibility – noble, serious, an actor's role – but his two great opportunities for dramatic monologues are pre-empted by Constanze's 'Martern aller Arten' in Act II and the lovers' recitative and duet in Act III. Then again, Mozart's enthusiasm for melodrama may have waned by 1782.

Different in style and conception though *Idomeneo* and the *Entführung* may be, Mozart's composing of the earlier Munich opera solidified his sense of dramatic architecture in a way very fruitful for his first great comic opera. Tonal planning represents one important area. Table 4 shows the opera's tonal layout.

Table 4 *Tonal plan of* Die Entführung aus dem Serail

ACT I

Overt.	1	2	3	4	5	6	7
C–c–C	C	g–B♭–D	F–a	A	C	B♭	c–C

ACT II

8	9	10	11	12	13	14	15	16
A	E♭	g	C	G	D	C	B♭	D–g–E♭–D

ACT III

17	18	19	20	21
E♭	b	D	B♭	F–C

Mozart has clearly organised the opera around the colour of his 'Turkish' key, C major, heard in a full third of the opera's numbers. He deploys it in much the same way he had used D major in *Idomeneo.* As in all his mature operas, both these works begin and end in the 'home' key, and, additionally, the first act (comprising the dramatic exposition) also begins and ends in this key. Further, the musical centrepiece, a dramatic *aria di bravura* for an anguished main character, asserts the prime key's tonal control over the mid-point of the drama in both operas – 'Fuor del mar' in *Idomeneo* and 'Martern aller Arten' in the *Entführung*.

The only other key areas employed more than once or twice in the *Entführung* are those flanking the home key – D major and B♭ major. D major is always invoked for its brassy brilliance – in the Presto concluding the duet of Osmin and Belmonte, in the sunny opening and closing sections of the quartet, and in two arias: Pedrillo's attempted bravado in 'Frisch zum Kampfe' recalls the key as well as the triadic assertiveness of 'Fuor del mar', and Osmin's maliciously gleeful 'O! wie will ich triumphiren' transposes the *stilo alla turca* into a key where Mozart could take advantage of Fischer's low D.

A very different but no less important role befalls B♭. Deeper, more sublime moments of self-expression are clothed in its duskier hues. Not by chance does it appear in the penultimate number of each act, where the drama reaches an important juncture for Belmonte and Constanze. All three numbers call for Mozart's beloved clarinets, which assume an ever greater and more idiomatic role in each. The key's rich poignancy and the relationship which it has coloured are both exalted in the lovers' most sublime musical moment, their farewell duet near the end of Act III as they await death at the Pasha's hands.

Mozart had earlier adumbrated the poetic–dramatic role of B♭ against brighter prime keys in Idomeneo's valedictory 'Torna la pace al core'. But in *Idomeneo* it yields immediately and without ceremony to the final Coro's burst of D major. In the *Entführung* Mozart moves more smoothly from the aura of B♭ left by the duet's last radiance through the prose dénouement into the Vaudeville's F major, then finally up another fifth to the brightness of C major. Some ignoramus altered the end of the Vaudeville in one important Viennese manuscript so that the concluding C major Janissary chorus is omitted and the opera instead ends in F major, as shown in Ex. 11.

Others did even greater violence to the opera's major constellation of essential tonalities. Singers without the range of Cavalieri or Adamberger sometimes transposed their arias downward, a practice which did not go unnoticed. One critic complained in 1835 that a Berlin Constanze had sung her arias down a whole tone, 'which did not work to advantage, especially in the splendid bravura aria

Ex. 11

'Martern aller Arten', transposed from a bright C-major into a muffled B-flat-major'.[10]

Architecture: aria structure

Within the opera's individual numbers Mozart explored a variety of shapes not only dramatically effective in and of themselves but also up-to-date sounding to Viennese ears. *Idomeneo* had revealed his mastery of the ternary aria form, which by 1781 had largely supplanted the *da capo* and *dal segno* patterns in serious opera. In the *Entführung* Mozart does not use it once, even for the most solemn pronouncements of Belmonte and Constanze.[11] For the opera's solo numbers he preferred instead three categories:

(1) *Song forms.* Mozart is at his most 'German' in following the

simple strophic pattern Bretzner had invited in both Pedrillo's Romanze (No. 18) and Osmin's Lied (No. 2). Both numbers, significantly, are sung as explicit songs in the drama. Elsewhere, ABA-type song forms (with or without textual repetition) appear in Belmonte's opening aria and the first Janissary chorus. The popular single-tempo rondo appears on two occasions: Blonde's second aria (ABABA, No. 12) and Osmin's last triumphant solo (ABACABA with coda, No. 19). The rondo principle also guides the drinking duet of Osmin and Pedrillo (No. 14).

(2) *Cavatina.* By this we refer to the eighteenth-century aria type composed of just the first part of the old *da capo* form, with its full text stated twice:

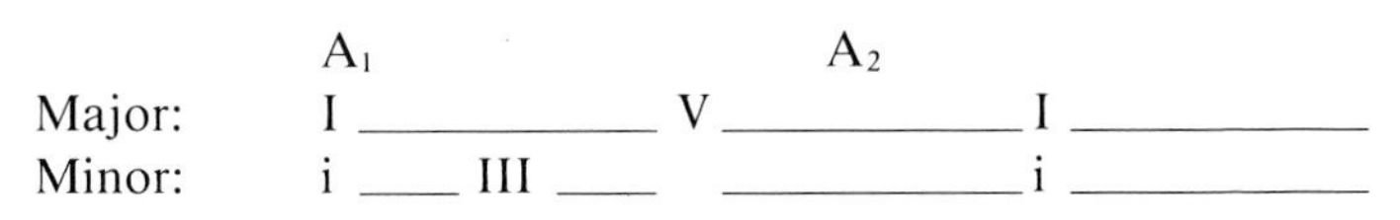

Osmin's sadistic 'Solche hergelaufne Laffen' (No. 3) illustrates the major form with added codas, and Constanze's exquisite elegy 'Traurigkeit' (No. 10) uses the minor-mode form after an introductory recitative. Mozart employs the cavatina in a more song-like fashion for Blonde's first aria (No. 8). His most innovative and masterly deployment appears in Belmonte's greatest aria, 'O wie ängstlich' (No. 4), to which we shall return.

(3) *Two-tempo structures.* It has been little remarked how frequently multiple-tempo patterns appear in the *Entführung* from beginning to end. One expects them in ensembles – especially larger ones concluding acts – but apart from such instances the *Entführung* includes seven further arias and duets which make significant formal use of multiple tempos. We have already discussed two of these, the Lied and duet of Osmin and Belmonte in Act I and the following aria of Osmin. Additionally all three of the penultimate B♭ numbers mentioned earlier use familiar two-tempo patterns of the day. The first, Constanze's 'Ach, ich liebte' (ABA′B, No. 6) shifts gears after the initial A section on a cue from the text ('Yet how quickly my joy vanished') and later repeats the opening material in the faster tempo with augmented note values to preserve its character. The other two numbers, Belmonte's 'Wenn der Freude Thränen fliessen' (No. 15) and the lovers' duet (No. 20), use the most familiar formal plan of all – a slow cavatina typically in gavotte rhythm (A_1A_2) followed by a new cadential section in the faster tempo, which is expanded on repetition (B_1B_2):

Slow		Faster	
A_1	A_2	B_1	B_2
I ——— V	I ———————	———————	———————

Mozart's most complex and unusual treatment of the two-tempo aria occurs in an equally serious context – in 'Martern aller Arten', the most controversial number in the opera.

'Martern aller Arten'

The show-stopping musical centrepiece of the *Entführung* poses many questions. When and why was it added? What are we to make of its unorthodox form, especially its extensive opening ritornello? Can it claim any dramatic relevance, or does it do no more than arrest the drama for the benefit of the prima donna?

That the aria and the dialogue supporting it were a Viennese interpolation is clear from comparison with Bretzner's libretto. Possibly the desire to get rid of the rather insipid rondeau text originally sung here by Constanze and Blonde prompted Stephanie and Mozart. At any rate, they moved in a direction precisely opposite to its passive expression of hope for release from torment in either this or a future life. Bretzner, in all fairness, was no prissy moraliser by nature. He very probably tailored this text and his pathetic, unassertive portrait of Constanze to the strengths of her creator at Berlin, Marie Niklas. 'As an actress everything strong, ponderous, or overwrought lies outside her sphere', wrote one Berlin theatre-goer of her in 1780. 'She makes great efforts to bring it off, but is not convincing. . . On the other hand, in every tender, innocent, merry, and good-hearted role she plays with great naturalness.'[12] He also remarked in this respect that 'her triumph is the rondeau'.

Elsewhere in the drama, Bretzner had provided for Marie Niklas's considerable vocal abilities in a way typical of Northern music-dramatic planning and squarely at odds with the *aria di bravura* as employed by Mozart and the Italians. At the very end of the drama – after all is said and done, and Selim has embraced Belmonte as his long-lost son and has welcomed Constanze as his daughter-in-law – Bretzner's heroine bursts into a paean of joyous rapture over the prospect of future bliss and the danger now safely passed. André set this aria (and indeed quite skilfully) as a ternary-form showpiece for Marie Niklas. It comes precisely where such an extended piece of virtuosic work could do no harm at all to the drama, already safely home to port.

Following north German precedents, Bretzner's earlier three-act librettos had also tucked the heroine's bravura aria in this same snug spot. They all trade in the unvaried theme of gratitude and joy (about the only one possible at this late moment). We can sense their dramatic irrelevance and uniformity in their poetic incipits, all introduced by the affective interjections Bretzner could seldom do without:

Das wütende Heer (1779): 'Ach! wie schwimmt mein Herz in Wonne'
('Ah! how my heart swims in bliss')
Der Irrwisch (1779): 'Ach! noch schwank ich halb im Taumel'
('Ah! I am still reeling, half delirious')
Belmont und Constanze (1781): 'Ah, mit freudigem Entzücken'
('Ah, with joyous rapture')

Stephanie's revision of the second of these operas for Umlauf in 1781 as *Das Irrlicht* had not included any attempt to relocate the bravura aria of the heroine Blanka, which stands as the penultimate number in the opera after a long prose dénouement. One suspects, in consequence, that Stephanie was urged to the excision of Constanze's similar aria in the *Entführung*, and the substitution of 'Martern aller Arten' earlier in the drama. It would appear entirely reasonable, then, to credit 'Martern aller Arten' to Mozart's account along with every other musical modification in the original libretto.

Since Stephanie and Mozart were not prepared to restructure Bretzner's plan in any major way, only a few opportunities for relocating an *aria di bravura* for the heroine presented themselves. The spot eventually selected offered several advantages. The uncongenial duet between Constanze and Blonde could be eliminated, the Pasha could be more fully integrated into the drama (in Bretzner's version he does not even appear in Act II), and the prima donna now had at least one scene in the opera crowned by an exit aria. Two infelicities had to be endured: (1) Cavalieri was now expected to sing two demanding arias in a row, something Mozart never asked of any singer before or after, and (2) a new and in some respects inconsistent side of Constanze's personality had to be developed very hastily in a preparatory interchange with the Pasha, in order to justify a spirited outburst from the otherwise dispirited Constanze.

So completely did Stephanie change Constanze's tone that her sudden self-possession and insolence toward her threatening wooer strikes us as nearly equivalent to Blonde's comportment toward Osmin in their altercation earlier in the act. (The temporary equivalence perhaps offers some small justification for the otherwise ridiculous decision of an 1859 Parisian production which assigned Constanze's great aria to Blonde.[13])

The text Stephanie composed for Mozart is in some ways an unusual one. Though originally printed in a single block of sixteen lines, it divides poetically and logically into three stanzas of six, four and six lines:

A.	
Martern aller Arten	Tortures of every kind
Mögen meiner warten,	May await me,
Ich verlache Qual und Pein.	I deride agony and pain.
Nichts soll mich erschüttern,	Nothing can unnerve me,
Nur dann würd' ich zittern,	I would only tremble
Wenn ich untreu könnte seyn.	If I could be untrue.
B.	
Lass dich bewegen,	Let yourself be moved,
Verschone mich!	Spare me!
Des Himmels Segen	May heaven's blessing
Belohne dich!	Be your reward!
C.	
Doch du bist entschlossen.	But you are determined.
Willig, unverdrossen	Willingly and unwearied
Wähl' ich jede Pein und Noth.	I choose every pain and misery.
Ordne nur, gebiethe,	Order away, command,
Lärme, tobe, wüthe,	Bluster, storm, rage,
Zuletzt befreyt mich doch der Tod.	In the end death shall free me.
(*geht ab*)	(*exit*)

Standard formal strategies in serious opera had all been developed with poetic texts of one or two stanzas in mind. A triple division, comparatively rare, always elicited unconventional responses from composers.[14]

The first six lines of Stephanie's poem establish Constanze's air of open defiance, of scorn for the horrors awaiting her, and of perpetual loyalty to Belmonte. The next four lines swerve suddenly to the supplicating tones familiar from her scene with the Pasha in Act I. Her pleas avail nothing, however, so the final sextain returns with even greater firmness to her original defiant resolve to embrace death.

Mozart's setting has some points of contact with a genre of two-tempo aria then at the beginning of its vogue among the Italians, which they and Mozart called simply 'Rondò':

Slower			Faster	
A_1	B	A_2	C_1	C_2
I	V	I		

Mozart's experimentation with various two-tempo patterns in the *Entführung* marks the beginning of his continuous cultivation of the Rondò throughout his final decade, both in operas and concert arias. Like the two-tempo pattern quoted earlier (p. 76), the Rondò involves a departure from the tonic only in the middle of the slow section. The same holds for 'Martern aller Arten', but in this case Mozart was much more directly concerned with the special rhetorical properties of the text itself:

Tempo:	Allegro							Allegro assai	Allegro	Allegro assai	
Section:	R_1	A		B_1		R_2	(B)	C_1	B_2	C_2	R_3
Text:		1–3	4–6	7–8	9–10			11–16	7–10	11–16	
Key:	I		–V/v	V			V/I	I			(I^6_4)

The contrasting B section of Stephanie's text presented a special problem. After beseeching the Pasha's mercy and invoking heaven's blessing if he grants it, Constanze cannot possibly return to the opening stanza. The third section supplies what is needed here: she reacts to his unresponsiveness to her pleas not with reiteration but with intensification of her original resolve. The last section (C) she states twice – a link to the two-tempo Rondò in its tonic orientation and cadential character. But Mozart turns this convention of repetition to poetic account by repeating Constanze's pliant supplications from the B section between the two statements of C.

The reinsertion of the B section, one might argue, points to the 'instrumental' dimension of this extraordinary aria, adumbrated and kept in our ears by the *concertino* of solo flute, oboe, violin, and cello. For the repetition of the 'Lass dich bewegen' section provides a sonata-like restatement in the tonic of the material previously presented in the dominant, something not considered necessary in the Rondò.

Still, there is nothing abstract about the dramatic role of the aria, which Mozart went out of his way to insert at the very mid-point of the opera, rather than simply set or substitute for Bretzner's *aria di bravura* at the end. 'Martern aller Arten' moves into clear dramatic focus if we hear it not as an expression of Constanze's defiance itself but of her struggle for this new-found spirit of resolve, a struggle which encompasses both proud derision and earnest pleading. If so, what better vehicle than the trappings of the concerto? The long opening ritornello, supposedly such a puzzle to auditors and such a headache to stage directors, offers a perfect medium for a preliminary instrumental–pantomimetic exposition of the struggle, for its own form anticipates the alternation of defiance and supplication co-existing in the embattled heroine. And the unusual reiteration of the B section in the middle of the Allegro assai – where an audience in 1782 would least expect it – carries the uneasy struggle of her two sides into the most conventional and, often, dramatically irrelevant section of this aria type.

Let us not overlook another struggle, the one going on in Selim's breast. He, too, plays his part in the aria, the opening words of which he himself supplied in the preceding dialogue. Mozart reflects the 'Eastern' harshness that temporarily holds sway over the Pasha's better instincts by injecting 'Turkish' elements into Constanze's aria. The very key of C major is one. Then there is the main motif, to which he himself has supplied the text – unisono, vigorously triadic, duple with firm downbeats, and invoking immediately the sharpened fourth degree (Ex. 12*a*). And just prior to it the ritornello's con-

Ex. 12*a*

Ex. 12*b*

cluding theme echoes the *échappée* embellishment of a descending scale heard in the Janissary choruses (Ex. 12*b*). The rising triad in the accompaniment heard in the C sections had already done service as an emblem of Osmin's spleen, and the riotous monophonic scales inundating the closing pages create an appropriately frenzied conclusion of a vaguely 'Turkish' stamp.

There is good dramatic sense beneath the introduction of these 'Turkish' tokens, as there is in every passage in 'Martern aller Arten', from its expansive opening ritornello to its high-voltage conclusion. The dark side of Selim's complex personality has evoked, in the best traditions of opera, a strong new voice in Constanze's hitherto melancholic personality. This new voice offered Mozart the opportunity to deal musically with a central relationship in the drama, to accommodate his prima donna, and to impress an audience he was anxious to win over.

The Romanze

On a far humbler level, Mozart displayed the same masterly creativity in dealing with song forms when he confronted and subtly modified two especially characteristic strophic genres in German operas of the day, the Romanze and the Vaudeville.

The first of these Mozart actually called by its French name, 'Romance', in the autograph score of the opera. But even though it was indebted to French example, the German Romanze had from its inception adopted a tone derived from a native forebear, the centuries-old tradition of the Bänkelsänger, or mountebank. It was the practice of these lowly, itinerant singers to set up platforms at fairs or in town squares and to recite their tragic and often grisly ballads as they pointed with a long stick to episodes depicted on a large piece of canvas or cloth. Usually, the Bänkelsänger sang about current events of a sensational nature – murders, suicides, or purported supernatural visitations, for example – while an accomplice sold printed copies of the poem and melody to the auditors.

As a literary category, the Romanze appeared in the 1750s as a mildly ironic imitation of this popular tradition. (The tone of a good Romanze was described in an important anthology issued in 1774 as one 'composed of caprice and drollery, of feigned simplicity and affected seriousness, sorrow, compassion, astonishment, and so forth'.[15]) It also absorbed features from similar poetry in France, Spain and England. Poets established a preference for the folk-like ballad metre, or four-line stanzas with first and third lines in iambic tetrameter and second and fourth in iambic trimeter. And when the Romanze found its way into German comic opera in the 1760s, librettists followed French models in fashioning the poem's narrative as a doublet of the opera's own plot. Usually a character sings the Romanze as an explicit song, warning someone, through the little story it tells, of the dark consequences a projected course of action might bring with it.

The primacy of the Romanze's narrative and its folkish character led most German composers to adopt a syllabic style in a simple strophic setting. They also overwhelmingly preferred moderate tempos – so much so that, as in the case of Pedrillo's 'In Mohrenland', a tempo designation might be omitted altogether. To varying degrees, these composers followed Rousseau's practical lead in trying to achieve the somewhat 'archaic' style he urged for a good *romance*. Various means were used – irregular melodic construction, frequent recourse to the minor mode, harmonic enrichment with secondary dominants and diminished chords, and modal degrees or modal ambivalence between major and minor.

As a literary phenomenon the Romanze was largely a northern product, but Austrian composers and audiences welcomed it in the librettos they imported from the north. Stephanie never thought to eliminate this popular item in any of the librettos he adapted, and in the *Entführung* he preserved Pedrillo's Romanze even though he dismantled the action ensemble in which it occurs.

Bretzner's 'In Mohrenland' does not confine itself simply to providing a narrative reflex of the opera's plot, as custom had established. It also creates a new role for this lowly genre as an ingredient in the elopement itself. Pedrillo, we learn, has been wont to sing such songs in the streets at night, so the Janissaries will take no particular notice of him. But tonight the completion of his song signals to Constanze and Blonde that they are to throw open their windows. Each passing stanza is an eternity to Belmonte, who breaks in after the second to urge Pedrillo to be finished quickly. By playing upon his nervous impatience, Bretzner quite cleverly turns the repetitive strophic structure of the Romanze to dramatic account.

The tense, expectant atmosphere urged an equivalent aura of hushed tension in the music. Mozart's setting is often described as loosely Moorish or exotic, in response to the text's subject, but the dramatic situation on stage provided the main impetus for the way he chose to interpret Bretzner's poem. Pedrillo is to accompany himself on the mandolin, and Mozart exploits this instrument not only with the 6/8 *alla siciliana* metre and pizzicato string accompaniment, but also with the choppy, hesitant one-bar cadences in B minor in the ritornellos, which imitate the trochaic metre characteristic of the up–down motion of a mandolin player's strumming hand (Ex. 13). Throughout the Romanze the trochees stand at metric odds with the firmly iambic tune which Pedrillo sings.

Ex. 13

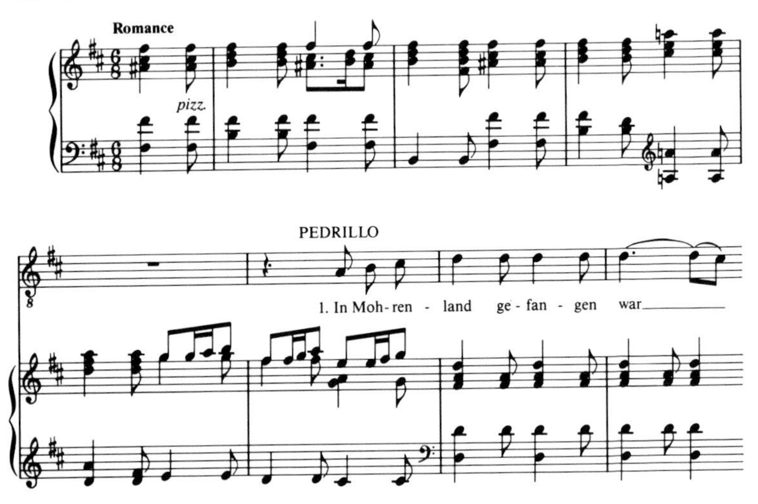

In some respects this tune follows the folk-like ways of earlier Romanzen, but not in the complexity of its motivic structure. As Ex. 14 illustrates, the rising and falling conjunct fourths which proliferate across the piece's surface appear as well on the song's highest architectural level. The descending B minor tetrachord (*B–F♯*) represents only one process, however: there is interwoven with it a concomitant descent from D to B, itself the handiwork of a pair of falling fourths – D to A, then C to G, outlined harmonically and melodically in Pedrillo's first two phrases.

Ex. 14

Another fourth continuing this pattern seems called for – it would complete both structural descents with its termini *B* and *F♯*. But Mozart compresses the up–down motion of the earlier phrases, clinging to G and then slipping down directly on to *F♯*. Possibly he had been led to this melodic plan by Bretzner's stanzaic structure, which adds an extra line of iambic tetrameter to the ballad metre scheme:

A	In Mohrenland gefangen war	(D major)
B	Ein Mädel hübsch und fein;	(A major)
A	Sah roth und weiss, war schwarz von Haar,	(C major)
A	Seufzt' Tag und Nacht und weinte gar;	(G major)
B	Wollt' gern erlöset seyn.	(F♯ minor)

The parallel *D–A*, *C–G* motion leaves us hanging on the 'added' fourth line disturbing the ABAB ballad metre scheme. Our ears still await a concluding trimeter 'B', rhyming with 'fein', to complete the stanza, which the compressed phrase resolving on to F♯ supplies.

The arrival on the dominant completes the descending tetrachord, but the other structural descent from *D* to *B* is left hanging until the jittery pizzicato ritornello sets in once again. As a result, the music's structure is at once open and circular. There is mild irony, too. The poem's final line brightly announces the successful escape of the imaginary knight and lady in its narrative, but Pedrillo's concluding 'hop-sa-sa' dies uneasily in the night air on the dominant, and the last statement of the ritornello stops skitterishly in mid-air, suspended in modal indecision between B minor and D major. The lovers in the opera, in fact, will fare far worse in their own escape attempt, which is set in motion by this ambiguous Romanze.

Belmonte

Now to the aria of Belmonte in A major. You know how 'O wie ängstlich, o wie feurig' is expressed. – And his beating 'loving heart' has also been portrayed already – with the two violins in octaves. – And it was written entirely for Adamberger's voice. You can see the trembling – irresolution – how his heaving breast rises, which is expressed by a crescendo – you hear the murmuring and sighing, expressed by the first violins with mutes and a flute in unison (26 September 1781).

With these appeals to seemingly naive pictorialism, Mozart described to Leopold the most revealing, characteristic and subtle of the arias in the opera – and one of the most beautiful as well. What kind of hero is Belmonte? Bretzner, in common with many librettists, looked upon a protagonist's first aria as the most important occasion for fixing his dramatic character. His Belmonte in this aria is a lover paralysed with hope and fear at the moment of seeing his beloved – an excruciating moment in this case, for he knows she will be in the company of her would-be lover.

Mozart had asked Stephanie to insert an earlier aria for Belmonte, which offers a preliminary glimpse of the ambivalence in his breast. Uncertain and tentative, and marked with skitterish dynamics, the melody of 'Hier soll ich dich denn sehen' opens up cautiously to its high *g′*. Its first note seems unsure whether it is to be crusis or anacrusis (Ex. 15); but then out of initial tentativeness blossoms

Ex. 15

instinctive lyricism, capped by the high *a′* of 'bringe mich ans Ziel'.

Mozart deepens and completes this preliminary portrait of his hero with 'O wie ängstlich'. So thoroughly does this aria describe Belmonte that for the rest of the drama he develops further only in ensembles (the quartet and lovers' duet). His two additional arias contribute nothing of dramatic relevance to his character, and in fact when the second (No. 17) is omitted, as often happens, No. 15 is usually plucked from its place near the end of Act II and substituted for it in Act III.

No such transference of 'O wie ängstlich' could possibly be contemplated, at least not without carting the preceding dialogue between Belmonte and Pedrillo along with it. Their interchange not only sets the stage verbally for the aria's poetic burden with Belmonte's exclamation, 'My heart is beating with fear and joy', but more importantly it sketches in the kind of young man who might find himself caught between these emotions.

The strength of Belmonte's ardent love for Constanze is also his weakness, for it makes him a hapless prey to pangs of jealousy and fear over her fidelity. It is up to Pedrillo to channel events, to invoke reality and pragmatism against his master's airy hopes and fears. As Sonja Riekmann has put it in a thoughtful study, 'However understandable Belmonte's anxiety may appear, it indicates a sentimental, undynamic nature. One gets the impression that without Pedrillo's power of action the prisoners would never get out of the seraglio.'[16]

'O wie ängstlich' is without doubt one of the most pictorial arias Mozart ever wrote. Scarcely a significant word escapes musical painting:

ängstlich (anxious) – open cadence, staccato, piano
feurig (fiery) – closed cadence, staccato, forte
klopft (beats) – violin figure, staccato[17]
liebevolles Herz (loving heart) – chromatic inflections, roulade on '-volles'
Zähre (tear) – trickle-down figure in first violins
Schmerz (pain) – deceptive cadence, V-♭VI
zittre, wanke, zage, schwanke (I shake, waver, hesitate, falter) – 'heartbeat' figure in minor with *fp* accents
es hebt sich die schwellende Brust (my swelling breast heaves) – murmuring demisemiquavers rising above a crescendo
Lispeln (whisper) – flute fluttering in demisemiquavers
Seufzen (sigh) – demisemiquaver fillips on weak beats
täuscht, Traum (deceive, dream) – augmented sixth chord

Mozart could indulge himself to such a degree because the pictorial technique, far from serving its own ends, acts as an ingenious psychological tool.

His letter of 26 September 1781, quoted above, spells out the factors uppermost in his mind – Adamberger's voice and Belmonte's irresolution. The two are not completely separate, however. The vocal writing in the aria suggests that Adamberger had a particular gift for singing expressive chromatic neighbours, appoggiaturas, and passing notes. These are precisely the ingredients Mozart had lavished on the role of Ilia in *Idomeneo*, suggesting a subtle parallel between her and Belmonte. His later arias, too, elaborate the same chromatic touches seen in 'O wie ängstlich' as an emblem of his hesitancy.

Musical indecision and wavering appear on several planes. At the beginning the dominant and subdominant jostle for control, both in the brief opening recitative and in the first two phrases of the aria, where after an open cadence on the dominant a mildly ungrammatical subdominant asserts itself and forms a plagal close (Ex. 16*a*). A hundred other composers of the day would probably have written a parallel second phrase here resembling the one proposed in Ex. 16*b*.

Harmonic irresolution appears several times in the aria after this. E major, heard in bar 28 as the dominant of A minor, converts abruptly to E minor. This turns out to be the subdominant of ii,

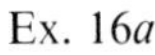

Ex. 16*a*

Ex. 16*b*

B minor, but the dominant of that key, to which Belmonte's heaving breast swells, decides to veer off to D major instead. Though highly irregular as the goal key of the first section, this subdominant could scarcely be bettered as an area for Constanze's imagined whispers and sighs.

In the second half of the aria tonal stability returns. But the text now appears disordered and with it the sequence of musical images traversed in the first half. The 'heartbeat' motif assumes complete control, substituting for other figures derived from it (as at 'Schon zittr' ich und wanke'). It participates as well in a final delightful allusion Mozart makes to the young lovers' predicament in the closing ritornello: Belmonte's heartbeats slowly die away beneath a reminiscence in the woodwinds of Constanze's whispers and sighs, the two of them separated, as it were, by a sustained tonic octave in the horns. Thus at the return to dialogue Mozart leaves us with a sort of musical preview of the uneasy scene that follows – Belmonte and Constanze finally together again, yet still separated by the presence of the Pasha.

Unity and coherence

Compared with other German operas of its day, *Die Entführung aus dem Serail* set new standards of musical ambition. A popular, apocryphal anecdote, first aired by Niemtschek in 1798, records a purported exchange between Joseph II and Mozart over the opera: 'Too beautiful for our ears, my dear Mozart, and monstrous many notes!' 'Exactly as many as are necessary, Your Majesty.' The tale fits neatly into the posthumous myth of Mozart the free artist on the outside of the Viennese musical establishment and ruled only by his innate genius. Its historical plausibility may be questioned on several grounds – it does not sort with Mozart's anxiousness to please the Viennese, with the musical concessions he admitted making to Caterina Cavalieri's 'geläufige Gurgel', or with the cuts in several numbers which he later sanctioned.

Apart from its suitability for the rites of Mozart-worship, the anecdote also thrived on the inability of many among the opera's initial auditors to grasp the music's psychological involvement in nearly everything that matters in the drama. The true subject of this brief conversation, if anything like it ever occurred, might well have been Mozart's accompaniments, perceived by many of his contemporaries as overwrought, distracting and difficult to absorb. Yet precisely here throbbed the very heart of Mozart's style – or, to push a metaphor, the diastole to the systole of the human voice which together create the sense of a living organism in each of his mature operas.

Actually, 'accompaniment' is too narrow a term for a complex of phrasing, harmonic rhythm, cadences, motivic structure, and dialogue with the instruments. Mozart used all these elements with unprecedented freedom and plasticity. For a brief illustration, we need look no further than his sublime setting of the first two lines of Constanze's meditation 'Traurigkeit ward mir zum Loose' in Act II (Ex. 17).

The first word means everything; its motif, announced ahead of time by the woodwinds, speaks all the more eloquently in that it is never used for anything else in the aria. The following nine bars explore three new motifs (*x*, *y*, *z*); each has its own rhythmic shape, but each also echoes the poignant upward leap of 'Traurigkeit'. Further, the half-steps that account for virtually all the voice-leading in the opening motto find their way back into our ears at every opportunity.

Ex. 17

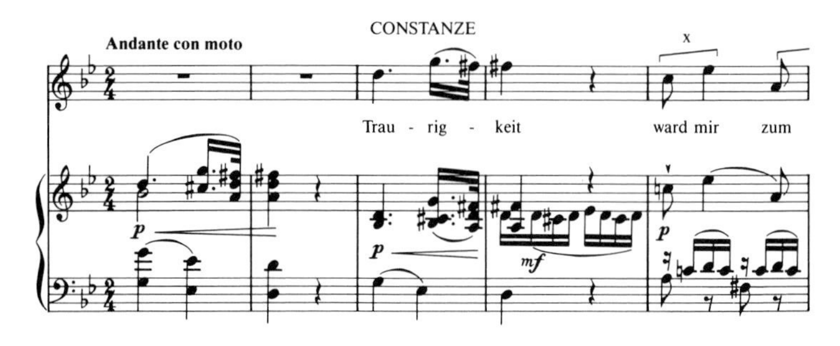
Andante con moto
CONSTANZE
x
Trau - rig - keit ward mir zum
p
mf

6
x′
y
y′
Loo - se, ward mir zum Loo - se, weil ich dir ent - ris - sen bin,
sf
p

11
z (≈ y′ inv.)
weil ich dir ent - ris - sen bin, weil ich dir,
ten.
f
sf
p

16
weil ich dir ent - ris - sen bin.

The unifying power of the strong opening gesture is apparent, yet the aria does more than languish in Constanze's 'Traurigkeit'. A striking pause and stern *D*'s from the woodwinds twice dramatise the cruelty of the 'Loose' ('fate') about which she complains. Similarly, mention of her being torn from Belmonte ('ich dir entrissen') inspires disruptions of her line. These linear disruptions complement other elements in Mozart's style – the varied harmonic rhythms used in each new bar, the sforzandi, the flexible phrase lengths (6–5–6, subdivided 2+4–2+3–2+2+2), and the cadence goals (i_6, ♭VI, i).

Now let us look at what André did with these same two lines (not an especially unfair comparison in this instance, since he too was setting Bretzner's verses for an accomplished soprano). Though a pleasant, competent eight-bar phrase, Ex. 18 falls woefully short of bringing to life Constanze's sorrow, much less anything that Bretzner's text is saying. Everything is squared off, the harmonies change regularly and predictably, the ii–I sequence falls right where we expect it, and for his cadences the composer can think of nothing

Ex. 18

more original than an open–closed pattern. Such a framework leaves no room for anything striking. How pallid and pointless the tonicisation of the subdominant (bars 6–7), compared with the sinking effect that reaches out for our sympathies from bars 15–17 of Mozart's setting! André opts at the beginning for the neutral up–down scurrying in conjunct motion which he had learnt from French melodies. By the time his Constanze gets to her sforzando leap in bar 11 it is too late for such a token gesture to mean much.

Psychologically and emotionally, Mozart creates vividly and specifically from text, character and situation, engaging the listener with every compositional detail. André, of whom northern operatic tradition demanded far less, demands less of us as well. One number readily blends into the next in his score. He cast his 'Traurigkeit' in rondo form, even though the succeeding duet is also a rondo. Most telling of all, the main theme of the aria is disturbingly similar to that of the preceding aria, which stands at such great spiritual distance from what Constanze sings (Blonde's 'Durch Zärtlichkeit und Schmeicheln', Ex. 19). After the initial upbeat of the earlier number,

Ex. 19

the recipe is much the same: it's up a fourth and down a sixth in stepwise motion, then on to a tonicisation of IV, correct the seasoning at once with a sharpened fourth degree, then end with a double appoggiatura, all without ever violating the control of duple bar groups.

To return to Mozart, we might recall here Dent's influential assessment of the opera as 'a succession of masterly and original numbers' with no real unity of style. His major criticism of the opera, embodied in this statement, clearly has nothing to do with the internal consistency and musical merits of individual items, nor their dramatic relevance, but rather with the overall impression they create as a group. Dent no doubt realised that the range of serious and comic in the opera was nothing extraordinary for the period. The real source of what dismayed him lies rather in the profusion of German, French, Italian and 'Turkish' elements which rub shoulders in the *Entführung*.

Mozart expended every ounce of his genius in tempering each one of these elements to fit clear and consistent operatic–dramatic ends. But there were clear limits set by the model he and Stephanie worked from; under these circumstances it was inevitable that incongruities would arise whenever Mozart's poetics of opera ran up against structures created for more modest musical accompaniment. Here, indeed, loomed the central aesthetic problem of the opera. Its stylistic diversity does not really lie between the individual musical numbers but between the competing claims of Mozart's music and Bretzner's dialogue. They are claims we must learn to live with. Any modern performance or analysis that fails to take the dialogue seriously does Mozart no great service and compounds the problems posed by the opera.

Modern critics have tried in various ways to analyse the inner coherence of the music, usually under the assumption that what lies between the opera's twenty-one numbers should be ignored as so much inert matter. They begin, of course, with the overture. Constantin Floros has charted a constellation of associations between the overture and several later numbers, which demonstrates nothing more than the motivic consistency of Mozart's 'Turkish' style.[18] Stefan Kunze objected to Floros's programmatic implications and preferred to view the overture as 'an autonomous instrumental composition', an emblem, in fact, of Mozart's commitment to 'musical autonomy'. Any hidden motivic connections with the opera are 'accidental'.[19] Kunze fails to acknowledge, much less explain, the overture's formal unruliness; its strong expressive contrasts he interprets with antiseptic detachment as 'the objective idea, as it were, of the theatre as comedy'.

Imagine, however, that you are a stage director entertaining the idea of raising the curtain with the first notes of the overture (as often happens these days). Now Kunze's pallid metaphor must be transformed. No disembodied play of ideas about 'the theatre as comedy' takes centre stage, but Belmonte, thrust into a menacing, exotic environment. Amid the disorderly racket of the overture's 'Turkish' sections, the hesitant, darkened anticipation of the hero's Lied emerges in C minor as a personality – as a complete, closed lyric utterance.

To be sure, in Mozart's own day our experiment would have raised eyebrows along with the curtain, which normally remained down for an opera's overture, no matter how closely tied its music might have been to the rest of the opera. Even so, Daniel Heartz has argued, Mozart's overtures from *Idomeneo* onward follow Gluck's directive in the preface to *Alceste* (1769) that an operatic overture should acquaint the audience with the nature of the action about to unfold – in other words, that it should act as the opera's dramatic argument.[20] In so doing it also adumbrates a unity of musical discourse which interacts with and deepens the dramatic unities, both the neo-Aristotelian ones of time, place and action (scrupulously observed by Bretzner) and more especially the all-encompassing one which superseded these three in the minds of theorists like Diderot, Mercier and Lessing – unity of interest.

Yet within the opera Mozart appears to carry on an especially brisk trade in elements that challenge our sense of stylistic well-formedness – contrast, disruption, tonal irregularity. In a play where East meets West the results could scarcely have been otherwise, given the Western stereotypes of Islamic personality traits current in Mozart's day. Disruption threatens whenever Osmin appears, and the consistency with which it does so is not only a reflection of his integrated musical personality but also a major factor in the unity of the opera's musical language. What the overture promises and Osmin embodies is sustained through each act, thanks to his enlarged presence, and achieves its full measure of dramatic integrity at the end in the most resolutely regular opera-ending item of the day, the Vaudeville.

A typical closing vaudeville in a French or German opera provides a stanza of text for each of the principals, each sung to the same folk-like tune. The text inevitably expounds a lesson learned or an insight gained from the action by each character. Each stanza ends with a refrain-like thought which all the singers repeat. Sometimes, as in the *Entführung*, a chorus follows the vaudeville.

Mozart did not set his Vaudeville and chorus in the same key, however, but rather reserved the opera's tonic C major for the perfunctory Janissary chorus tacked on to the F major Vaudeville. Hans

Keller has pointed to the seeds of this 'progressive' tonal plan in the Vaudeville tune itself (Ex. 20). Following tradition, first Belmonte and then Constanze repeat the melody exactly, but Mozart modified the second five-bar phrase for Pedrillo and Blonde (Ex. 21). Keller saw the significance of this in more forceful linear motion to the dominant (preparing for its promotion to tonic in the chorus).

Actually, the modification possesses more immediate import. The new phrase, less ornate and thus more appropriate to the servant pair, acts to strengthen the hold of the pitch *A* and of the subdominant area of the anticipated dominant (IV/V and ii_6/V). These features pave the way for even more radical changes at precisely the same spot in Osmin's contribution to the Vaudeville. Begrudgingly he has sung along with the others in praise of his master at the end of the first three stanzas, but he bursts out in fury at the end of Blonde's stanza, of which the last lines were clearly not intended for repetition by everyone but as a parting poke at Osmin:

> (*auf Osmin zeigend*)
> Denn seh' er nur das Tier dort an,
> Ob man so was ertragen kann.

> (*pointing to Osmin*)
> For just look at that animal –
> can such a thing be endured?

As happened so often before, Osmin loses control. He browbeats the music into a new key, metre and tempo with a recapitulation of the only thing he can think of in such a state – the tortures that the lovers have coming to them, first catalogued in 'Solche hergelauf'ne Laffen' in Act I.

Yet even this final outburst has been carefully prepared, not just by the earlier occurrence of the passage but also by the Vaudeville itself. In his rendition of its melody, Osmin simply exaggerates, as he has done all along, what he hears these foreign dogs sing – in this case the *A* dwelt on earlier by Pedrillo and Blonde in the tune's second phrase (see Ex. 21). By twisting its harmonisation into an augmented sixth chord[21] he propels the piece into A minor instead of the anticipated C major (Ex. 22). Keller would like to hear this

Ex. 22

A minor 'retrospectively invested with the significance of a relative minor' once we get to the C major chorus, but its most meaningful relationship is the immediate one with F major, both here and in Osmin's aria in Act I. This may well be why Mozart chose F major for the Vaudeville in the first place.

Stephanie re-established the number's tone with a final sextain for all four lovers. Apparently he intended it to be sung, like their earlier separate stanzas, to the Vaudeville's melody. But such a crudely managed return right after Osmin's dramatic exit would have been a capital musical blunder. The lovers recover F major only by degrees. At first Constanze's line hangs with uncertainty on to Osmin's repeated *A*'s. Eventually her brooding sforzando half-step *A*–*B*♭ yields to a high *f*′. From here Constanze slowly sinks down through the octave, withholding a solid tonic *f′* until the very end of the sextain. Nothing is as hateful as revenge, the lovers observe. In contrast, to be humane and to forgive selflessly is the province of only great souls. With this drawing of the moral to the accompaniment of simple, heartfelt chordal four-part harmony Mozart anticipates the spirit of *Die Zauberflöte* more clearly than anywhere else in the opera.

When the lovers finally rejoin the Vaudeville, they pick it up right where Osmin had broken off in his wrath – with the closing epigram. And once recovered, fittingly, it is turned against him. The Pasha's noble example should be as obvious to the virtuous-minded as the return to the tonic, and

> Wer diese nicht erkennen kann,
> Den seh' man mit Verachtung an.
>
> (Let him who cannot recognise this
> be looked on with scorn.)

In a blaze of sunlight the Janissary chorus bursts in to second the lovers' praise. Although in a new key, their exaltations do not come out of nowhere, for Constanze's descending octave has established an important motivic link with the opening of the C major chorus (Ex. 23). The *C–B* figure adds a subtle tonal link, too – invoking for

Ex. 23

a moment the dominant of *F* Lydian, with the sharpened fourth degree characteristic of Mozart's 'Turkish' style.

The descending octave at the beginning of the chorus has another antecedent as well. It recalls and completes the *C* to *G* to *D* falling fourths left unresolved by the opening phrases of the overture (Ex. 24). Heartz has indicated in the other mature operas of Mozart 'cases where a late or even final musical gesture in the work became, at some point in the compositional process impossible to determine, the nucleus of the overture'. Here in the *Entführung* the gesture we

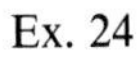

Ex. 24

have cited creates not only architectural but also poetic closure. The restoration of moral order acknowledged by the Janissaries in their own key and in their own way completes a kaleidoscope of human states to which Mozart had applied his 'Turkish' style throughout the opera.

6 *The opera in performance*

On 30 May 1782, exactly ten months after having received Bretzner's libretto from Stephanie, Mozart played the final act of *Die Entführung aus dem Serail* to Countess Thun-Hohenstein and Constanze Weber. Four days later the opera was put into rehearsal. Mozart looked forward eagerly to the première, which came six weeks later on 16 July. An influenza epidemic had closed the theatre for a week during rehearsals, and the National Singspiel no doubt needed every minute to prepare this difficult but promising new score.

The current season had not begun auspiciously that April. In each preceding year the enterprise had put three new operas into production at the start of the season, between Easter and the end of May, but this year only two appeared. Stephanie, now in sole charge of operatic productions, first scheduled Maximilian Ulbrich's *Das blaue Schmetterling*. Despite an attractive score and a strong cast (including Dauer, Fischer, Teyber and Aloysia Lange[1]), the opera disappeared after only three performances.

Next the National Singspiel tried something unprecedented in its brief history – an opera buffa sung in Italian, Sacchini's *La contadina in corte* (first performed at Rome in 1765 and already familiar to Vienna from a 1768 production at the Burgtheater). Stephanie no doubt knew of strong local prejudice in favour of Italian opera, although his own avowed sympathies lay with German opera, and he may already have got wind of the emperor's plans to reinstate a troupe of Italian singers at the Burgtheater. Further, Sacchini's opera allowed him to take advantage of Antonia Bernasconi, whom Gluck had enticed to Vienna for *Alceste* and *Iphigenia auf Tauris* in late 1781. But *La contadina in corte* had to be dropped after only two performances when Bernasconi took a leave of absence in April. No other new work was ready to put into production, so older fare already in the repertory had to fill out three dreary months until Mozart's opera was ready.

Première and early Viennese performances

The playbills went up for *Die Entführung aus dem Serail* on the day of its première, 16 July 1782, but they provided Viennese theatre-goers with less than the usual information about the new production (see Plate 2). An empty space stood where the casting formerly appeared, for Joseph had ordered that, as of the beginning of the new season, the names of the singers were no longer to appear on posted playbills. Mozart's name was included, albeit inconspicuously, but Stephanie's was omitted entirely. Not so that of the fashionable Bretzner. Contrary to normal practice, it received special typographical prominence.

Mozart's letters to his father speak of cabals in the audience at the first performance. None the less, full and ever more enthusiastic houses greeted each new performance despite the intense summer heat:

> [My opera] makes such a sensation that nobody wants to hear anything else, and the theatre is always swarming with people. – Yesterday it was given for the fourth time and Friday it will be given again. – Still – it wasn't so long ago that the whole world was claiming that I'd made enemies of the professors of music and other people, too, with my boasting and criticising! (31 July 1782)

An earlier letter contains revealing comments on those in attendance at the second performance: 'The theatre was almost fuller than the first time. – The day before a reserved seat was not to be had either in the *parterre noble* or the third floor; and no loges, either' (20 July 1782). Beyond the financial dimension of this popularity (1,200 florins in two days), Mozart meant also to convince Leopold of the enthusiasm for his opera among every class of spectator. The loges were almost exclusively the property of the high aristocracy at the Burgtheater; the *parterre noble* contained in addition artists, intellectuals and military officers; a more middle-class group peopled the *dritter Stock* (third floor), also the station of many critics and connoisseurs. (See Plate 3 for a contemporary illustration of the interior of the Burgtheater during a musical performance, where all these locations can be observed.) Mozart does not mention the cheaper and rowdier gallery at all. Its intemperate and ill-timed applause 'was accorded no special value, if indeed it was rather not generally considered painful or even dishonourable'.[2]

Mozart followed the fortunes of his opera closely and did not fail to pass on to Leopold any special mark of distinction it brought him. On 6 August the National Singspiel performed the *Entführung* at

Neues Singspiel.

Die Kaiserl. Königl. National - Hof - Schauspieler
werden heute Dienstag den 16 July 1782 aufführen:

(Zum erstenmal)

Die Entführung aus dem Serail.

Ein Singspiel in drey Aufzügen,
nach Bretznern frey bearbeitet und für das k. k. Nationalhoftheater eingerichtet.

In Musik gesetzt vom Herrn Kapellmeister Mozart.

Die Bücher sind beym Logenmeister für 17. kr. zu haben.

Der Anfang ist um halb 7 Uhr.

Plate 2 Playbill for the première of the *Entführung*

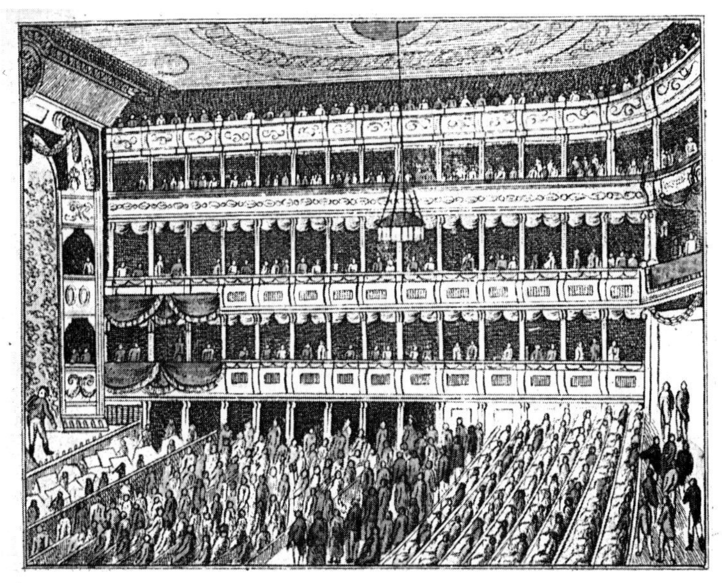

Plate 3 Interior of the Burgtheater (coloured engraving, anonymous)

the special request of old Gluck, who paid Mozart many compliments on his achievement – a descendant of his own *La Rencontre imprévue* – and invited the young composer to dine at his home. In October the Russian guests of a year earlier, in whose honour the opera had originally been planned, returned from Italy and were fêted with a performance. 'I considered it advisable to return to the keyboard and to conduct, partly to reawaken the orchestra, which had drifted off to sleep a little, and partly (since I am here) to show myself to the sovereigns in attendance as the father of my child' (19 October 1782).

With the end of the National Singspiel in early 1783, an Italian company took over at the Burgtheater. A private German company performed at the Kärntnerthor Theatre, which Joseph brought under imperial control and protection in September of 1785 as 'die Deutschen Hof-Operisten'. The sort of rivalry he apparently hoped would improve the German troupe's fare sprang up between them and the 'Italiänische Hof-Operisten'. The Germans scheduled a revival of the *Entführung* on 25 November 1785 so as to compete with the Viennese première of Francesco Bianchi's *La villanella rapita*, given by the Italian troupe (the version they produced included two substitute ensembles by Mozart). On the playbill, which carried the offerings of both companies, the Germans added a note to lure those undecided between the two productions: 'Madame Lange will appear in the theatre again today for the first time after her long illness in the role of Constanze.'[3] Aloysia scored a great triumph. Early the following year she chose the opera for her benefit evening at the Kärntnerthor, with her brother-in-law conducting.

Other productions during Mozart's lifetime

Mozart kept track of the successes scored by the *Entführung* not only at Vienna but also on other German stages. A list of premières during the opera's first decade appears in Table 5. Niemtschek witnessed the first performance outside Vienna, in Mozart's beloved Prague. The enthusiasm it kindled in connoisseur and amateur alike was soon to be duplicated elsewhere:

> It was as if what had hitherto been heard and known here was no longer music! – Everyone was ravished – everyone felt amazement at the new harmonies, the original, yet unheard of treatment of the wind instruments. Now the Bohemians began to seek out his compositions, and already in that very year one began to hear Mozart's keyboard works and symphonies in all the

Table 5 *First performances of* Die Entführung aus dem Serail *during Mozart's lifetime*

Date	Place	Company
16 Jul 1782	Vienna (Burgtheater)	National Singspiel
autumn 1782	Prague	Karl Wahr
8 May 1783	Warsaw (in German)	Lubomirski
22 Jun 1783	Bonn	National Theatre (Grossmann)
2 Aug 1783	Frankfurt am Main	Grossmann
25 Sep 1783	Leipzig	Bondini
25 Nov 1783	Warsaw (in Polish)	National Theatre
18 Apr 1784	Mannheim	National Theatre
16 Oct 1784	Karlsruhe	Appelt
24 Oct 1784	Cologne	Grossmann
5 Nov 1784	Vienna (Kärntnerthor)	E. Shikaneder–H. Kumpf
17 Nov 1784	Salzburg	Johann Ludwig Schmidt
1784	Schwedt	Court Theatre
12 Jan 1785	Dresden	Bondini
1 Mar 1785	Riga	Court Theatre (Brandes)
1 Apr 1785	Munich	National Theatre
4 Apr 1785	Weimar	Bellomo
24 Apr 1785	Aachen	Johann Heinrich Böhm
26 May 1785	Kassel	Grossmann
13 Jun 1785	Pressburg	Count Erdödy
Jul 1785	Erlangen	Johann Ludwig Schmidt
1 Aug 1785	Nuremberg	Johann Ludwig Schmidt
19 Aug 1785	Augsburg	
25 Nov 1785	Vienna (Kärntnerthor)	German Court Opera
3 Dec 1785	Mainz	Grossmann
5 Jul 1786	Rostock	Johann Tilly
17 Jul 1786	Altona	Johann Tilly
summer 1786	Pyrmont	Johann Heinrich Böhm
12 Apr 1787	Hanover	Grossmann
18 Jun 1787	Hamburg	Friedrich Ludwig Schröder
24 Aug 1787	Breslau	Barbara Wäser
23 Nov 1787	Koblenz	Johann Heinrich Böhm
15 Jun 1788	Graz	Waizhofer
16 Oct 1788	Berlin	National Theatre
early 1788	Budapest	Heinrich Bulla
1788	Brunswick	Grossmann
1788	Hildesheim	Grossmann
1788	Königsberg	Schuch-Ackermann
7 Jan 1789	Lübeck	Grossmann

Table 5 (*cont.*)

Date	Place	Company
14 Apr 1789	Bamberg	concert performance
27 May 1789	Ofen	Humbert Kumpf
1790	Hermannstadt	Christoph Ludwig Seipp
Jan 1791	Amsterdam	Jakob Johann Albert Dietrich
Mar 1791	Erfurt	

better concerts. From now on the preference of the Bohemians for his works was decided. The greatest connoisseurs and artists of our native city were also Mozart's greatest admirers and the most ardent heralds of his fame.[4]

The success of the *Entführung* nearly everywhere was unprecedented for a German opera from Vienna and, as Niemtschek suggests, played a decisive role in the founding of Mozart's reputation beyond the imperial capital. The Bonn National Theatre production of the *Entführung* in 1783 represented a particular compliment to its power: the director and conductor were none other than Grossmann and Neefe, author and composer of the opera's kindred spirit *Adelheit von Veltheim*, still a popular opera on many German stages. This production must have been young Beethoven's earliest experience of Mozart's dramatic genius.[5]

Soon the opera touched others who played a part in its background and genesis. When the Bondini company brought it to Leipzig for the Michaelmas Fair in 1783, Bretzner himself – to whom we shall return in a moment – must have heard Mozart's music for the first time. At the Schwedt Court Theatre in 1784 Marie Niklas, the soprano for whom André had composed the part of Constanze in Bretzner's *Belmont und Constanze*, took the same part in Mozart's version.[6]

Viennese works soon came to dominate the musical repertories of nearly all German stages. The Döbbelin company at Berlin turned suddenly and decisively to operas from Vienna in 1783. All six of the new works introduced there that year had seen their premières at the Burgtheater. But *Die Entführung aus dem Serail* was not among them. The opera could scarcely have been unknown in musical circles there; in fact, the score had been ordered soon after the first performances at Vienna. On 25 September 1782 Mozart wrote to his father:

The Prussian ambassador [Johann Hermann von] Riedesel has informed me that he has been instructed by the Berlin Court to send my opera *Die Entführung aus dem Serail* to Berlin; therefore I should have it copied, and the payment for the music will soon follow. – I promised right away to have it copied. – Now since I don't have the opera, I would have to borrow it from the copyist, but that would be quite inconvenient, for I can't be *sure* of keeping it for three whole days, since the emperor often sends for it (as happened only yesterday) and then again it is often given, for in fact it has already been presented ten times since the 16th of August [*recte* July]. – Hence my idea would be to have it copied at Salzburg, where it could be done more secretly and cheaply! So I ask you to have it copied out in score right away – neatly, but with all haste, too.

Earlier Mozart had sent his autograph of the opera to Leopold,[7] from which a copy for Berlin was eventually made. There, however, the opera languished for nearly six years until 16 October 1788, when it became the first Mozart opera ever staged at Berlin.

During the early 1780s the Prussian court exercised no direct control over the offerings of the Döbbelin company, although Crown Prince Friedrich Wilhelm took a warm interest in their activities. Döbbelin, we should remember, not only had André's original setting of *Belmont und Constanze* already in his repertory in 1782, he also had its composer as his music director until 1784.

In 1786 the former crown prince, now King Friedrich Wilhelm II, created the Berlin National Theatre out of the Döbbelin troupe, and a year later he demoted old Döbbelin from its directorship. Shortly thereafter Mozart's opera finally had its Berlin première in a production honouring the birthday of the Prussian queen on 16 October 1788. As occasionally happened elsewhere, it appeared on the playbill under the older title *Belmont und Constanze* – a familiar one to Berliners, of course, but now 'performed for the first time after the composition of Herr Mozart'.[8]

Perhaps the decisive factor in the National Theatre's decision to mount Mozart's opera was the arrival in early 1788 of the tenor Friedrich Carl Lippert, enticed from Vienna by an extraordinarily high salary, who took the part of Belmonte. The opera created no immediate sensation at Berlin, but held its own and eventually paved the way for *Figaro* and *Don Giovanni*, which arrived in 1790. During his visit in 1789, Mozart himself attended a performance of the *Entführung* by the Berlin National Theatre on 19 May at the cramped Theatre in the Gendarmenplatz.

Bretzner's reaction

In 1868 Constant Wurzbach published a document, almost surely spurious, said to have appeared in a Leipzig journal some time in 1782. It reads simply: 'A certain man in Vienna by the name of Mozart has had the audacity to misuse my drama *Belmonte und Constanze* as an opera text. I hereby most solemnly protest this infringement on my rights and reserve the right to take further action.' It is signed 'Christoph Friedrich Bretzner, author of *Das Räuschgen*'.[9]

This documentary imposture, surprisingly, has been uncritically reprinted by nearly all subsequent scholars who have written about the *Entführung*. Yet it is clearly suspect on several counts. First of all, Bretzner never referred anywhere else to *Belmont und Constanze* as a 'Drama', but always called it an 'Operette' or 'Oper', for that is what is was from the beginning. Further, although he is indeed 'the author of *Das Räuschgen*', he did not publish this comedy until 1786, four years after Wurzbach's 'protest' was supposedly issued. (This play was, incidentally, the work for which Bretzner was best known in the nineteenth century.) It is also noteworthy that the 'protest' does not bear a date, contrary to all the other public pronouncements, notices, and letters Bretzner published. And if the usurpation of *Belmont und Constanze* so irked him, why did Bretzner never utter a word against the adaptations of his other librettos for Vienna?

The fabricator of this document was probably playing on the fact that Bretzner had actually singled out the *Entführung* from these other reworkings in an authentic notice, dated 27 April 1783 and published in the Berlin journal *Litteratur- und Theater-Zeitung*. Here, however, he took aim not at Mozart but at the 'unnamed person in Vienna' who had not only adapted 'my opera, *Belmont und Constanze*' for the National Theatre there, but more importantly 'has allowed the piece to be published in this altered form'.[11]

Clearly, Bretzner's primary concern was for the literary integrity of what was passed off under his name, and that meant the printed word first and foremost. He felt so strongly about this particular revision because, thanks to Mozart, the changes and additions here were far more thoroughgoing than in other Viennese adaptations of his texts.

'Since the alterations in the dialogue are not considerable,' Bretzner notes, 'I shall pass over them completely. But at the same time the adapter has inserted a group of songs in which quite heartbreaking and edifying little verses occur. I would hate to snatch the glory of his labour from the amender, so I find myself compelled to specify the lyrics inserted by him according to the Viennese edition and Mozart's composition.' After listing Stephanie's additions Bretzner offers an excerpt from the new Act II finale with the ironic remark: 'That's what I call improving!'

Bretzner himself, or someone sharing his contempt for Stephanie's poetic contribution, seems to have taken the matter further by attempting a laundering of the new verses. A revised version of the poetic texts of the *Entführung* arose in north and central Germany with emendations of some sixty-four lines of text, without disturbing a note of Mozart's music.

The corrections to the Viennese text in this version are far from random. Not a single line from any of the nine numbers by Bretzner is rewritten. All sixty-four new lines replace ones originating with Stephanie; in fact, only one of his thirteen contributions escapes some stylistic cleansing. Although the evidence is mostly circumstantial, one is tempted to attribute these changes to Bretzner himself. Who else would have wished to make so airtight a distinction between his and Stephanie's contributions, which he had publicly condemned?[12]

Immediate critical response to the *Entführung* suggests that these poetic revisions were labour ill bestowed, for Mozart's music preoccupied everyone. Goethe reacted negatively to it at the first performance of the opera by the Bellomo company at Weimar in 1785:

> Everyone was in favour of the music. The first time it was performed indifferently; the text itself is very poor and even the music I could not swallow. The second time it was performed very poorly and I actually walked out. Still the work held its own and everyone praised the music. When they gave it for a fifth time, I went once again. They acted and sang better than before, I put the text out of mind, and now I understand the difference between my judgment and the impression of the public, and I know how things stand with me.[13]

But by the 1790s things stood differently with Goethe. As director of the Weimar Court Theatre from 1791 to 1817 he saturated the programmes with performances of operas by Mozart and other Viennese composers, and the *Entführung* stood high among the most popular, outshone only by *Die Zauberflöte* and *Don Giovanni*.

In 1788 Baron Adolf von Knigge offered his own assessment of the relative merits of the text and music of the *Entführung* after witnessing the Grossmann company's production at Hanover on 3 October:

There is not much to be said about the piece itself. The invention of the intrigue and the way it is elaborated do not have the value of novelty, and neither does one encounter poetic beauties here; still, one is happy not to feel the advantageous impressions the music makes weakened – as in Italian opere buffe – by purposeless, insipid twaddle and tomfoolery.[14]

A backhanded compliment at best for the poet, yet Bretzner himself eventually adopted a more modest estimation of the role his texts played in the operas he helped create, a change in heart accompanied by a decisive turn toward Italian models and methods. Mozart was a part of his aesthetic. His references to the composer during these years breathe an admiration which runs counter to the trumped-up tone of Wurzbach's spurious 'protest'. In 1787 Bretzner published a novel in three volumes, *Das Leben eines Lüderlichen* (based on Hogarth's 'The Rake's Progress') which mentions *Le nozze di Figaro* several times and even quotes one of Cherubino's arias. In 1794 he translated *Così fan tutte* into a widely adopted German version. Finally, in 1796 Bretzner published a set of three new, utterly Italianate librettos with a preface in which he acknowledges the modest role a text now plays in an opera. Yet he also slyly vaunts the part his most famous libretto had played in Mozart's career as a dramatic composer: 'Mozart first became known to the German stage through the *Entführung*. Perhaps one of these pieces, too, will awaken some yet slumbering musical genius, and then I shall at least have the honour of having awakened him.'[15]

The nineteenth century

After the widespread popularity which the *Entführung* enjoyed on German stages during the last two decades of the eighteenth century, it encountered less and less enthusiastic audiences as operatic sensibilities changed rapidly during the nineteenth century. Sporadic interest, often accompanied by nationalistic pride, prevailed at home, while abroad the opera was twisted, pillaged, padded or ignored.

The statistics available on the relative popularity of the *Entführung* at Vienna and Berlin in comparison with Mozart's other major operas can perhaps be taken as symptomatic of its standing throughout German-speaking lands. Table 6 illustrates its uncertain position – not quite up to the high orbit achieved by *Figaro*, *Don Giovanni* and *Die Zauberflöte*, but considerably ahead of *Così fan tutte*, *La clemenza di Tito* and *Idomeneo*.

Table 6 *Mozart's major operas at Vienna and Berlin*

Opera	Vienna Staatsoper 1869–1953	Berlin 1788–1952
Idomeneo	20	15
Die Entführung aus dem Serail	241	380
Le nozze di Figaro	511	803
Don Giovanni	455	780
Così fan tutte	117	139
La clemenza di Tito	8	72
Die Zauberflöte	503	905

Sources: Emil Pirchan *et al.*, *300 Jahre Wiener Operntheater* (Vienna, 1953), pp. 256–65
Hugo Fetting, *Die Geschichte der deutschen Staatsoper* (Berlin, 1955), p. 271

German writers and critics mirrored the variability of responses from audiences in the theatre during the nineteenth century. Many of them, down to the present day, have taken up Carl Maria von Weber's evolutionary view of the opera's place in Mozart's oeuvre.[16] Others often echo the nationalistic tone adopted in 1826 by a Munich theatre-goer, who described the opera as 'the youthful, powerful work of a great genius, completely calculated for German voices and at the same time a challenge that no Italian throat can meet, especially when our fiery director bids his masses of sound advance in quick-step'.[17]

The first major Viennese revival of the century occurred in May of 1808.[18] The cast was a strong one, particularly Antoinette Campi (Constanze) and Ignaz Karl Dirzka (Osmin). The playbill for a performance on 17 September carried the remark: 'The aria inserted into Act III is also by Mozart', one of the first references to long-term dissatisfaction, at Vienna and elsewhere, with Belmonte's aria, 'Ich baue ganz auf deine Stärke'. A Viennese libretto from the end of the century omits it and appends a note to Belmonte's aria 'Wenn der Freude Thränen fliessen' in Act II: 'The insertion from *Così fan tutte* is often sung in place of this aria.'[19] The aria referred to here, almost certainly Ferrando's 'Un' aura amorosa', is possibly the same one indicated in the 1808 playbill. This production also set a precedent for later Viennese revivals in cutting three arias from the second act – 'Durch Zärtlichkeit und Schmeicheln' (Blonde), 'Traurigkeit ward mir zum Loose' (Constanze), and 'Frisch zum Kampfe' (Pedrillo).

The *Entführung* fared well for all of 1808 at the Kärntnerthor, but by spring of the following year it played to mostly empty houses. Johann Friedrich Reichardt believed the music suffered most from the torpor and inertia of the orchestra, filled with old, infirm men who had long deserved to be pensioned off, but who remained in service to make ends meet in inflationary Vienna.[20] Ten days later he reported from Prague the complaint of music lovers that the public there had lost their taste for the *Entführung* and *Titus*, both of which were given in very mediocre performances.

The opera proved more durable at Berlin, which saw a spate of productions in 1829, 1831, 1835, 1837 and 1844. At the last of these a reviewer observed that 'although the piece is out of date and uniform, and also lacks big ensembles, nevertheless the magic of Mozart's melodies and the beautiful instrumentation continue to interest the friends of music uncommonly'.[21]

In this production both 'Wenn der Freude Tränen fliessen' and 'Traurigkeit ward mir zum Loose' were dropped from Act II. Similar cuts and adjustments were apparently a common feature everywhere in Germany and Austria. A perfectly competent soprano, Caroline Seidler, omitted 'Martern aller Arten' at Berlin in 1831. In other performances a considerable cut of eighty-two measures in the middle of this aria was frequently taken; it can be traced back to the earliest manuscript copies of the music at Vienna and appears in many early piano–vocal scores.[22]

German modifications amounted to mere child's play, however, next to the mutilations the opera suffered abroad. Paris first heard the opera in relatively undistorted form, initially in a French translation by Moline in 1798, then three years later when a German troupe headed by a certain Haselmayer set up a stage there, which they named Théâtre Mozart. They opened it with the *Entführung* on 16 November but dropped the opera after the third performance owing to lack of interest. Soon after the company fell apart.[23]

In 1859 Prosper-Pascal revised Mozart's opera so that it could be given by the Théâtre Lyrique in tandem with Weber's *Abu Hassan*. Berlioz described the results:

Die Entführung, according to nearly all our fellow music critics, has been performed at the Théâtre Lyrique with the most *scrupulous fidelity*. All that was done was to put into two acts a piece that had three, *to invert the order of succession of several pieces, to subtract a grand aria from the role of Madame Meillet* [Constanze] *in order to give it to Madame Ugalde* [Blonde] *and to put between the two acts the famous Turkish March, so familiar to pianists who play Mozart.*

Well! Very good! So that's what one is supposed to call *scrupulous fidelity*![24]

On the other hand, Berlioz was not about to dispense unconsidered praise for the object of these distortions simply because it was by Mozart. Much in the music kindled his disdain. The overture, for instance, struck him as a piece of capital naiveté, which Leopold ought to have ordered the (supposedly) seventeen-year-old Wolfgang to burn. Berlioz may have been inclined to ignore prosaic facts which might dampen his poetic fulminations, yet he was not alone, then or now, in his stern judgment of the opera: 'There is a multitude of pleasant little vocal pieces, it is true, but also a multitude of formulas which one regrets to hear so much the more because Mozart used them later in his masterworks, and because today they are a veritable thorn in our sides.'

Berlioz could not stand a note of Blonde's music and found little enough to admire in Osmin's. On the other hand he lavished praise on Belmonte's arias and particularly on the lovers' recitative and duet: 'The sentiment is very beautiful, the style much more elevated than everything preceding it, the form grander, and the ideas masterfully developed.' The serious, the noble, the sublime, the touching – these qualities alone moved Berlioz here. In this he differed little from many of his contemporaries. Consider, for example, how a critic took Gluck himself to task as early as 1807 for the same failings in *La Rencontre imprévue*:

This opera is an aesthetic monster. It has the character of neither comic nor tragic music. It wavers between power and vacuity, between expression and lack of clarity. Gluck seems apparently to have ventured here into a sphere that did not accord at all with his serious talent. As a result, in the light genre he is insufferable, but in contrast the least passage tending toward the tragic is brought off in a masterly way.[25]

The *Entführung* reached London on 24 November 1827, the last of Mozart's major operas save *Idomeneo* to do so. *Don Giovanni*, the only one to have fared well there, suffered the same grotesque disfigurement accorded to most foreign operas which found their way to Covent Garden for performance in English. In adapting the *Entführung* for this stage, William Dimond saw at once several severe deficiencies: a cast of only five, a single action, virtually no change of scenery, and a Pasha who inexplicably forgives everyone at

Plate 4 Anton Brioschi, the garden of Pasha Selim, Act II (Vienna, 1906)

the drop of a hat. This 'would never have satisfied John Bull', he remarked in his preface. So he reshaped the plot around a much larger cast and a series of subsidiary episodes.[26]

Dimond transferred the action to 'a Greek Island in the Archipelago', no doubt with current events in mind. The War of Greek Independence, which raged throughout the decade, had reached a critical stage in 1827. Greeks increasingly looked to England for support, and the English, we may be sure, had not forgotten the philhellenic idealism of Lord Byron. Increasingly harried and declining inexorably in power, the Ottomans finally suffered a crushing defeat at the hands of a combined British, French and Russian flotilla at Navarino on 20 October 1827, just a month prior to the appearance of *The Seraglio* at Covent Garden.

Near the beginning of the drama, just after Belmonte (posing as a painter) has landed, Dimond introduces a happy band of islanders and an elderly Greek landowner, Eudoxius ('Of Good Name'). Belmonte sets about painting the ruins of a temple to Bacchus, and Eudoxius praises his respect for their Greek heritage:

> These monuments of former glory, are to the poor bondsman, the lonely evidence that his country *once* was free. – We feel a melancholy pleasure in beholding them. – Yet, ah! the bequests of science to an age of barbarism, are but as the eternal lamps within Egyptian sepulchres, which vainly *gleam* upon the slumberers, but cannot *warm* (p. 5).

Just then Osmyn arrives with a detail of labourers; he points to a piece of sculpture and gruffly orders them to 'strike down that trumpery', which he intends to use to fill up a ditch behind the Pasha's stables.[27]

As might be gathered, Dimond followed Bretzner's plot only loosely. Blonde, now Pedrillo's sister, openly foments rebellion among the women in the seraglio. She has fallen in love with an Irish doctor who attends the Pasha, named O'Callaghan. Ibrahim himself, 'born of Christian parents; carried into slavery, when a child – and since risen to rank thro' his wonderful valour in the field', keeps and reveres a bracelet bearing his mother's portrait. The discovery of a duplicate in Constanze's possession leads to the revelation that he and she are brother and sister.

Dimond's refabrication required some additional music, much of it for the new characters. A certain Christian Kramer, Master and Conductor of His Majesty's Band, supplied the necessary items and also laid hands on what was kept of Mozart's score.[28] Some of the

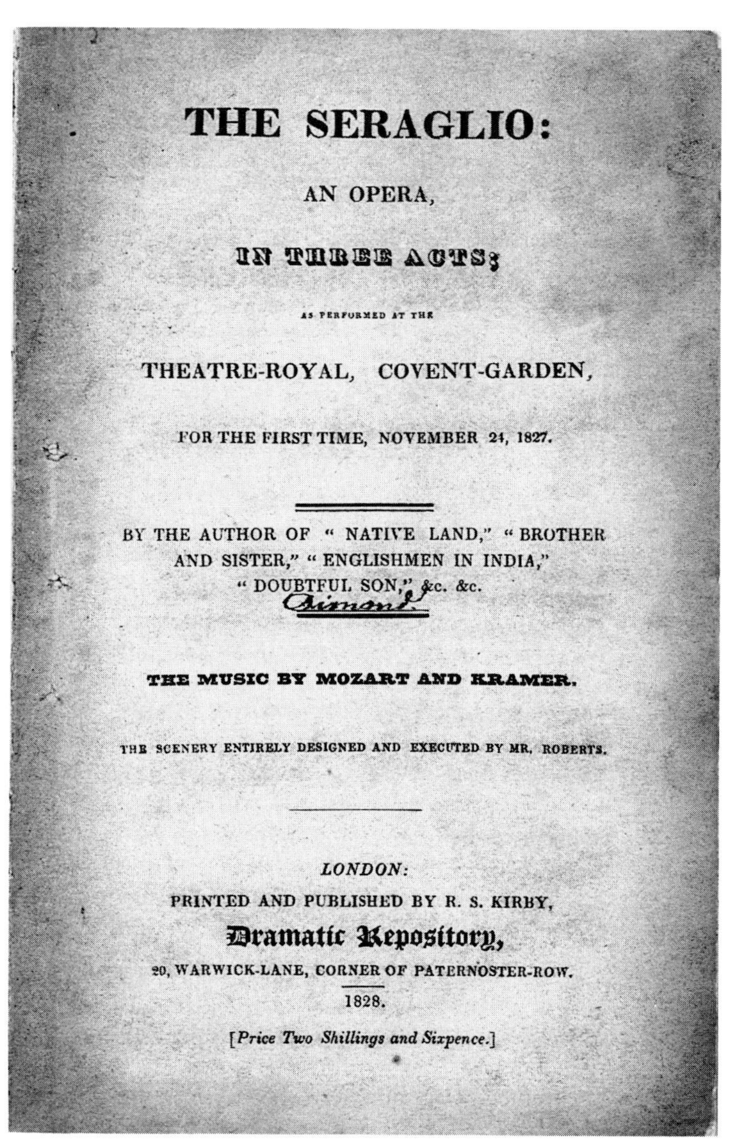
THE SERAGLIO:

AN OPERA,

IN THREE ACTS;

AS PERFORMED AT THE

THEATRE-ROYAL, COVENT-GARDEN,

FOR THE FIRST TIME, NOVEMBER 24, 1827.

BY THE AUTHOR OF "NATIVE LAND," "BROTHER AND SISTER," "ENGLISHMEN IN INDIA," "DOUBTFUL SON," &c. &c.

THE MUSIC BY MOZART AND KRAMER.

THE SCENERY ENTIRELY DESIGNED AND EXECUTED BY MR. ROBERTS.

LONDON:

PRINTED AND PUBLISHED BY R. S. KIRBY,

Dramatic Repository,

20, WARWICK-LANE, CORNER OF PATERNOSTER-ROW.

1828.

[*Price Two Shillings and Sixpence.*]

Plate 5 Title page of William Dimond's adaptation *The Seraglio* (Covent Garden, 1828)

best music, much of it Belmonte's, disappeared altogether from *The Seraglio*: 'Solche hergelaufne Laffen', 'O wie ängstlich', Durch Zärtlichkeit und Schmeicheln', 'Frisch zum Kampfe', 'Wenn der Freude Thränen fliessen', 'Ich baue ganz auf deine Stärke', and 'O! wie will ich triumphiren!' In two of these cases, Kramer actually had the cheek to set his own music to texts that Dimond had clearly translated for use with Mozart's original music – Belmonte's 'O wie ängstlich' and 'Ich baue ganz auf deine Stärke'.

In Italy, no performance of the *Entführung* seems to have occurred in any form before the middle of the twentieth century. Several Italian translations appeared quite early, however, and the opera was given in Italian both at Brooklyn (16 February 1860) and Covent Garden (9 June 1881).

A medical doctor resident in Milan named Peter Lichtenthal advertised in 1840 his own two-act modernisation of the *Entführung*, which he had prepared in hopes of having it performed at La Scala. 'Now in order to fit the *Entführung* to contemporary Italian theatrical taste,' he wrote, 'it was necessary above all to create grand vocal numbers and to give the Pasha a significant singing role, and consequently to rework completely the text, which is based on a very simple plot, and to deck it out with Mozart's music.'[29] This last involved putting texts under the inevitable *Alla turca* movement from the piano sonata in A major, K.331; the great concert aria written for Nancy Storace, 'Non temer, amato bene', K.505 (minus the obbligato fortepiano part); parts of movements from two sonatas for piano and violin, K.379 and K.526; both the trio (K.480) and quartet (K.479) that Mozart had written for Bianchi's *La villanella rapita*; and the larghetto section from the Act II finale of *Don Giovanni* ('Or che tutti, o mio tesoro').

For some spots Lichtenthal simply could not find anything in Mozart that would do, so he turned to the works of Joseph Weigl and Peter Winter (variations on 'Ein Mädchen oder Weibchen'). Lichtenthal himself composed the necessary recitatives. Of Mozart's original numbers only a few had to be left out, the adapter noted with pride – Belmonte's third aria, all three of Constanze's, and both of Blonde's as well as her duet with Osmin!

Lichtenthal twice played through this new version at the piano with Mozart's son Carl Thomas, long established at Milan, 'and each time he expressed his satisfaction with it. The fact that it has to date still not been performed at La Scala may be attributed on the one hand to the lack of adequate singers and on the other to a reason that is better passed over here'.[30]

Modern productions

How to deal with the *Entführung* as a part of today's repertories? Production practices of the present century do not hold out a simple answer to this problem, although beyond the surface variety of approaches lies a consensus that Mozart's music alone makes the opera worth doing. Here, too, lies the greatest stumbling block: so completely does Mozart's music seem to monopolise attention that any serious dramatic use of music's sister arts normally strikes listeners as obtrusive.

Certainly the simplicity of Bretzner's plot has proved fatal to taking the development of the intrigue seriously. By the late nineteenth century, much of the dialogue seemed superfluous when measured against the demands of musical continuity, and so directors routinely cut it to the bone, even at Vienna. In many productions, cavernous stages created for grand opera contrast grotesquely with the modest dimensions of the opera. What odd remnants of serious drama remain for the eye often disappear with stage settings that approach the exotic in the spirit of nursery tales.

In contemporary practice both fanciful and realistic stage design and costuming have proved effective, but only when they avoid mannerism or symbolic exegesis. It is as though audiences feel instinctively protective of the work's seeming innocence. Often a theatre's dimensions dictate which approach works best. At the intimate Glyndebourne stage in 1956 Oliver Messel's new sets and costumes were much admired for his having 'evidently gone to authentic Moorish designs, miniatures and carpets and buildings, and looked at them not only with his own eyes but also with those that an eighteenth-century scene-designer might have brought to them. The result is bewitching.'[31] A year later at Rome a riot of fantastical exotica struck another English critic as 'overpoweringly pictorial'. The visual display 'all but swamped the characters, but succeeded in making a Mozartian *singspiel* come alive on a huge Verdian stage'.[32]

Jean-Pierre Ponelle indulged his passion for 'historicised' period pieces with a controversial production of the *Entführung* at Cologne in 1974. The proscenium area of an eighteenth-century theatre in High Baroque style formed part of the stage set, including the imperial box,[33] occupied by Joseph II himself. In the course of the opera the emperor leaves his box several times to double as Pasha Selim in the drama, a parallel long overworked in the secondary literature on the opera and which here turns art into artifice.

Similar attempts to do the opera in anything other than a straight rendition have usually met with disapproval, if not the actual booing heard at Cologne. The work does not suffer witty ploys well, either – Blonde's reading *The Times* under a Union Jack (Glyndebourne, 1972), the substitution of mime for much of the dialogue (Rome, 1973), a game of hide and seek round a bubbling fountain to fill out the ritornello of 'Martern aller Arten' (Munich, 1967), or a tasteless burlesque of a Turk at prayer (English National Opera, 1975 and later).

What slender occasion the opera affords for political–social interpretation has been exploited to the full, especially in Germany. The notorious Frankfurt production of Ruth Berghaus in 1981 radicalised what many consider Mozart's most harmless operatic masterpiece: she 'rejected for the first time the usual oriental fairy-tale scenery and in its place presented a psychological arena of cut-off, isolated bourgeois characters'.[34] Even on a more conventional plane, August Everding's version at the Munich National Theatre in 1980 capitalised with chilling timeliness on the American hostage crisis in Iran. Selim, restrained and clad in white during Act I, donned a black costume redolent of the Ayatollah Khomenei for his confrontation with Constanze in Act II, culminating in his threat of 'tortures of every kind'.

Salzburg has provided the most striking exception to the opera's apparent stiff-necked resistance to modern interpretative sophistications – the celebrated shadow-box version Giorgio Strehler first put before audiences at the third Salzburg Festival in 1965 (see Plate 6). Strehler exploited the small dimensions of the Kleines Festspielhaus not for intimacy of contact but rather for the exquisite artificiality of a miniature and of the theatre as theatre. Even those expecting something novel were taken by surprise:

> Never before has one seen a German Singspiel in the form of a Turkish opera so thoroughly formalised, stylised, so extensively abstracted from all sense of *milieu*. Luciano Damiani's décor consists of nothing more than two narrow vertical walls with oriental architectural forms, sketched as if with silver pencils, and a pellucid backdrop before which the singers positioned on the unlit apron for their arias stand out like silhouettes – shadow figures to Mozart's music.[35]

Not surprisingly, such a production teemed with pantomime. Viewers were particularly struck by the innovative stylisations which Strehler's fundamental conception invited. 'Sabres and clubs flew through the air just when required by Osmin, and what an idea to

Plate 6*a* Giorgio Strehler (Salzburg, 1965): Quartet-finale, Act II

Plate 6*b* In front of Pasha Selim's palace at the seashore, Act I

have Pedrillo's two wine bottles brought in a sedan chair!' And in Act III, 'How does one abduct a respectable young lady? Logically, as happens here, where she hands the cavalier all her belongings, including hat box and canary cage, from the ladder.'[36]

So successful did Strehler's version prove that the Festival remounted it seven times during the next decade. Only two seasons after its première it was already being referred to as a 'classic'. In 1969 Florence imported it for the Maggio Musicale Fiorentino festival, and three years after that it triumphed at La Scala. What a contrast to twenty years earlier, when the opera was first produced at La Scala in Italian! This grandiose production survived only four nights, despite Maria Callas in the role of Constanze (see Plate 7).

A little earlier, the *Entführung* made a very belated appearance in 1946 on yet another large, traditionally-minded stage, the Metropolitan Opera in New York. Sung in an English translation by 'a cast scarcely better acquainted with the work than the public',[37] it was abandoned after only four performances.

Outside Austria and Germany, no stage has shown greater partiality to the *Entführung* this century than Glyndebourne. During its first four seasons, devoted exclusively to Mozart's mature operas, the Festival included the opera three times. Artistic Director Carl Ebert often played Pasha Selim himself in these early productions. 'His only action out of character,' recalls Spike Hughes, 'disapprovingly noted by many of the critics, was the lapse of good manners which led him to walk off the stage during the orchestral introduction to "Martern aller Arten" and so leave the unfortunate Constanze talking to herself instead of to the character to whom her defiant outburst is addressed.'[38]

Strehler, too, later struggled with this notorious spot and arrived at an even more drastic solution – he had the curtain dropped at a signal from the Pasha for the entire orchestral ritornello. A ballet filled out this troublesome stretch of music at Rome in 1973. At Covent Garden in 1938 Sir Thomas Beecham introduced his own solution: he simply moved the aria from its place in the middle of Act II to just after the abduction scene in Act III, where it makes no dramatic sense at all (she sings it alone on stage, before Selim is awakened with the news of the escape attempt) and seriously undermines the expressive force of the lovers' recitative and duet.

As often as not, the *Entführung* is done in the vernacular when produced outside Germany and Austria. Sadler's Wells has used Dent's translation since 1952 under the title *The Seraglio*, and vari-

Plate 7*a* Ettore Giannini, Gianni Ratto and Leonor Fini (Milan, 1952): Pasha Selim's garden, Act II

Plate 7*b* Closing scene, Act III

Plate 8*a* In front of Pasha Selim's palace at the seashore, Act I (New York, 1946)

Plate 8*b* Emmanuele Luzzati, in Pasha Selim's palace, Act II (Glyndebourne, 1968)

ous other English and American companies have experimented with over half a dozen other translations and adaptations. New texts often go hand in hand with new interpretations. When David Pountney rewrote the opera's dialogue for Scottish Opera in 1978 he considerably expanded the role of Pasha Selim, something which was quite the opposite of the ruling trend towards near annihilation of his verbal presence. During 'Martern aller Arten' the ladies of the harem formed a circle round Constanze in a show of feminist defiance.

The opera's closing message of clemency and understanding may seem of slightly worn estate today, but it was at least noted when by chance the *Entführung* was staged at the Vienna Staatsoper in 1979 before Jimmy Carter and Leonid Breznev during the SALT II summit meetings. Perhaps even more eloquent in historical perspective was a performance in Turkish which took place inside the Topkapi Palace at Istanbul in 1973, the first theatrical presentation of any kind within its walls. At the end of the opera each member of the chorus released a white dove.

Notes

(See the following Bibliography for complete citations of the works mentioned in abbreviated form here.)

1 Introduction

1 All quotations from the letters of Mozart and his family in this volume are newly translated from the complete edition of his *Briefe und Aufzeichnungen* published by the Internationale Stiftung Mozarteum Salzburg. In the text, passages from the letters are identified by date only.
2 Baron Adolf von Knigge saw Mozart's opera in a production by the Grossmann company at Hanover in 1788. He passed on the judgment of the troupe's music director, Bernhard Anselm Weber, who deeply admired the score but also judged it 'too serious here and there for the subject of a comic opera; in many otherwise masterly passages it approaches too much the style of serious opera, and since other really comic numbers differ all too markedly from this, unity of style is consequently lacking' (*Dramaturgische Blätter*, p. 23). Dent, in *Mozart's Operas*, 2nd ed., calls it 'an opera which is a succession of masterly and original numbers, but taken as a whole has no unity of style' (p. 73), and even suggests that the distractions of Mozart's estrangement from Leopold over his engagement to Constanze Weber very possibly had a hand in the work's poor planning and inconsistency of style.
3 *Sämtliche Schriften von Carl Maria von Weber*, ed. Georg Kaiser (Berlin and Leipzig, 1908), p. 303. (See also Weber, *Writings on Music*, pp. 264–5, for another translation of the complete text.) Weber published his discussion of the *Entführung* in the Dresden *Abendzeitung* on the eve of a production under his direction by the Royal Court Theatre on 17 June 1818.
4 *Skizze von Wien*, p. 316.
5 *Aus dem Josephinischen Wien*, ed. Richard Maria Werner (Berlin, 1888), p. 92.
6 Lange, *Biographie*, p. 47. The remark refers to an incident which occurred around 1771. Lange fell into a quarrel with Stephanie over the proper costume for a role he was playing in a certain scene. When Stephanie insulted him in the presence of the other actors, young Lange seized him by the throat. The author of the play intervened, 'perhaps more for the sake of his piece than for that of Stephanie'.

7 In June of 1781 there were very few published German librettos in four acts. I know of only six. Apart from two of no literary merit whatever, three of them are magic operas (a translation of Favart's *La Belle Arsène*; Graf von Spaur's *Der Schiffbruch*, reminiscent of Shakespeare's *Tempest*; and two translations of Marmontel's *Zémire et Azor*). The other is the most significant German rival to Bretzner's text among Turkish operas, G. F. W. Grossmann's *Adelheit von Veltheim*.

2 Conception and creation

1 *Joseph II., Leopold II. und Kaunitz: Ihr Briefwechsel*, p. 92. Joseph replied, 'With regard to the opera seria from Italy, it is too late to procure anything good, and besides it is such a boring spectacle that I doubt I'll ever resort to it' (p. 101).
2 Internal evidence suggests that this realisation probably came after the new scenes in Act II, surrounding 'Martern aller Arten', had been added. At the end of this interpolation Selim remarks, 'With harshness I've got nowhere – nor with entreaties. – Well then, what threats and pleas can't do, cunning will have to accomplish.' And yet no such exertion of the Pasha's wits occurs in the rest of the opera. A perfect venue, however, would have been provided by the 'entirely new intrigue' Mozart had asked Stephanie to create for the beginning of Act III, at a time he was still hoping to set Bretzner's 'charming quintet' as the finale of Act II (letter of 26 September 1781). The sequence of events suggested here is in harmony with Mozart's apparent overall strategy of setting the opera straight through from beginning to end and dunning Stephanie for changes as he went along.
3 *Sämtliche Singspiele*, 'Vorrede'. The entire preface has been reprinted by Renate Schusky, *Das deutsche Singspiel im 18. Jahrhundert* (Bonn, 1980), pp. 91–7.

3 Oriental opera

1 *Islam and the West*, pp. 273–4.
2 *Humanität und Kreuzzugsideologie um 1780*. Wilson has provided an English version of the substance of his argument pertaining to opera in a later essay, 'Turks on the Eighteenth-Century Operatic Stage and European Political, Military and Cultural History'.
3 Little serious work on the literary sources of the *Entführung* has appeared since the extensive yet uncritical work of Walter Preibisch, 'Quellenstudien zu Mozart's "Entführung aus dem Serail"'.
4 Parallels between Mozart's opera and the Menander fragment *Misoumenos* are drawn by Hans Jörg Schweizer, 'Bassa Selim', in *Sodalitas Florhofiana*. Another classical philologist, Cesare Questa, does the same for Plautus's *Captivi* in his *Il ratto dal Serraglio: Euripide, Plauto, Mozart, Rossini*, pp. 87–9.
5 The complete one-act play is printed in *Mozart-Jahrbuch 1978/79*, pp. 74–88.
6 Goldoni's comedy *L'impresario di Smirna* (1775) offers a good example.

A rich Turk tries to establish an Italian opera company at his theatre but the vanity of the singers he has engaged destroys the enterprise.

7 Bretzner's 'Extract from a Letter to Herr André', dated 4 October 1780, appeared in the Berlin journal *Litteratur- und Theater-Zeitung* 3 (1780), p. 672. He was obviously concerned about what audiences there would think of his new libretto once they had seen Grossmann's, which is indicative of the esteem he attached to his German opera as a literary work. A reviewer of the première of André's setting claims in the 7 July 1781 issue of the same periodical to have seen Bretzner's text at André's 'over a year ago' (4 (1781), p. 427).

8 *Dramaturgische Fragmente*, Vol. 4, p. 1002. Schink's comments on Mozart's music, as he himself admits, are those of a rank amateur who cannot even read music. He does, however, claim authority as a dramatic critic, and he goes on in the passage cited to censure Stephanie's new ending for yet another reason: 'Worst of all is that through this emendation the reason Bretzner had made his Pasha a renegade completely disappears and so makes the emendation even more unnatural.'

9 The simile must not be strained too far, however, for religious differences do not play any direct role in the dénouement, contrary to what one often reads. The Pasha dispenses his clemency with ill-concealed contempt for Belmonte's father and for the comportment of the young lovers, who have much yet to learn from his example. 'Tolerance' in the Josephine sense – freedom of worship, equality of social and political opportunity – does not enter into the matter.

5 The musical language of the opera

1 We shall use inverted commas around 'Turkish' to distinguish Western imitations from authentic Turkish music. In addition to the dissertation by Miriam Whaples, cited below, see Eve R. Meyer's article '*Turquerie* and Eighteenth-Century Music'.

2 *Ideen zu einer Ästhetik der Tonkunst*, ed. Ludwig Schubart (Vienna, 1806), pp. 330–1.

3 'Exoticism in Dramatic Music, 1600–1800,' unpublished Ph.D. dissertation, Indiana University, 1958, p. 156.

4 'Exoticisms in Mozart', p. 330. Szabolcsi does not insist upon a Hungarian character or provenance of such tunes, 'which seem to have preserved genuinely Turkish march or dance melodies that actually existed and were heard in this form'.

5 Erich Schenk appeals to modal interplay between C major and A minor in a desperate and overpoweringly unconvincing attempt to prove that a curious 'Dervish Dance' published at Vienna in 1781 inspired Mozart's first Janissary chorus ('Zur Entstehungsgeschichte von Mozarts "Entführung aus dem Serail"').

6 *Beschreibung einer Reise*, Vol. 4 (1784), p. 559.

7 *Sämtliche Schriften*, Vol. 1, p. 329.

8 *Aus dem Josephinischen Wien*, p. 105.

9 In bars 34–6 Mozart writes an especially pungent progression on the ritornello's bass pattern (*B*♭–*C*–*D*–*G*): i^{6}_{5}–♭II_{6}–i^{6}_{4}–V_{7}–i. Only the NMA

edition has printed the passage as Mozart wrote it. In his prefatory notes Gerhard Croll argues persuasively for the authenticity and propriety of the tonic minor seventh chord on *B*♭, which all previous editions had softened to a secondary dominant of iv with a *B*♮ in the bass.

10 *Allgemeine musikalische Zeitung* 38 (1835), p. 45. He added that the lead tenor also sang Belmonte's opening aria in B♭ rather than in C.

11 Mozart does use a variant of ternary form in the overture, with the B part in the tonic minor. However, the pattern he follows here is more likely to derive from Grétry. The overture to *L'Amant jaloux* (1778), for example, also includes a slow middle section in the tonic minor between exposition and reprise. Grétry availed himself of this plan in several overtures, the earliest of them *L'Amitié à l'épreuve* of 1770.

12 *Gallerie von Teutschen Schauspielern*, pp. 105–6.

13 Prosper-Pascal, who concocted this version for the Théâtre-Lyrique, provides his 'J'aurai donc enfin vengeance' with no dramatic context whatever – Blondine simply walks on to an empty stage and sings it. He adds the marginal comment that it could as easily be sung by Constance, 'selon les convenances locales, c'est-à-dire selon la chanteuse' (*L'Enlèvement au sérail, opéra comique en deux actes* (Paris, 1859), p. 30).

14 The most celebrated example of a three-part aria in the century was Metastasio's 'Se cerca, se dice' in *Olimpiade* (1733), discussed in *The New Grove*, s.v. 'Aria', Vol. 1, p. 578.

15 [Cajus Hirschfeld,] *Romanzen der Deutschen* (Leipzig, 1774), p. xxiv–xxv. He goes on to say, 'This tone comprises, together with the adventurous nature of the material, the most essential part of the Romanze's character.'

16 *Mozart: Ein bürgerlicher Künstler*, p. 90.

17 Mozart had recently used the same heartbeat figure in the exquisite E♭ major Adagio of the Serenade in B♭ major, K.361 (the so-called 'Gran Partita'), begun at Munich and completed at Vienna in the first half of 1781. Klaus Jungk points out the appearance of a similar figure in the aria 'Agita il petto' from *Lucio Silla* (*Tonbildliches und Tonsymbolisches in Mozarts Opern*, p. 66).

18 'Das "Programm" in Mozarts Meisterouvertüren'. The one connection Floros draws between the overture and a non-'Turkish' number is also the least convincing. He claims that the opening of the overture is related to the motif associated with the words 'Nur ein feiger Tropf verzagt' in Pedrillo's aria 'Frisch zum Kampfe'. The figure there is far more obviously akin to the opening of the Act IV finale in *Le nozze di Figaro* ('Pian, pianin le andrò più presso').

19 *Mozarts Opern*, p. 192. 'The search for relationships of motive and content between overture and opera,' Kunze remarks elsewhere, 'distorts one's eye [!] for what is intrinsic' (p. 189). Wagner, on the other hand, saw a very close connexion: 'It is impossible to hear [this overture] in a lively performance in the theatre without immediately being compelled to deduce with the greatest exactitude the character of the drama it introduces' (*Gesammelte Schriften und Dichtungen*, ed. Wolfgang Golther, 10 vols. (Berlin, n.d.), Vol. 1, p. 195).

20 'Mozart's Overture to *Titus* as Dramatic Argument', p. 29.

21 Hans Keller ('The *Entführung*'s Vaudeville', p. 311) smugly points out 'the consecutive fifths which the direct resolution on the dominant common chord necessitates here', apparently not having paused long enough to consult the full score, where they are carefully avoided. (Mozart forces Osmin off his reciting-note *a* up to *c′* for a moment in order to escape the parallel motion.) All piano-vocal scores of the opera, including the one based on the Neue Mozart-Ausgabe, introduce the parallel fifths into the voice-leading at this spot.

6 The opera in performance

1 The complete cast appears in Michtner, *Das alte Burgtheater*, pp. 119–20. Ulbrich's autograph score (now at the Gesellschaft der Musikfreunde in Vienna) carries a slightly different casting inside its front cover, including Adamberger rather than Dauer in the role of Don Eugenio. (Earlier in the year, Joseph had required that every role in a play or opera given by the National Theatre be double cast.) Thus the entire singing cast of the *Entführung* except possibly Cavalieri were involved in this new production at the beginning of the 1782/3 season.
2 Otto Schindler, 'Das Publikum des Burgtheaters', p. 53. In the later 1780s Pezzl also complained of a portion of the parterre which had adopted the nasty, ill-mannered habit of 'clapping their plebeian applause' every time an attack on the aristocracy occurred in a play (*Skizze von Wien*, p. 316). Although a presence in the theatre, these were not the ranks on whom the success of the *Entführung* depended, or from which the 'cabals' attending its première emanated.
3 Austrian National Library, Theatersammlung. During the same season the German company revived two other successful operas from the National Singspiel's last years, Umlauf's *Das Irrlicht* and Gluck's *La Rencontre imprévue*. Mozart's sister-in-law had quickly achieved even greater renown than Cavalieri as her 'alternate performer' in the role of Constanze. She frequently sang it on her artistic tours through Germany during the 1780s.
4 Quoted by Teuber, *Geschichte des Prager Theaters*, Vol. 2, p. 84.
5 Certainly Pedrillo's Romanze 'In Mohrenland' must have been in his mind when he wrote the B minor 'Minnelied' (sub-titled 'Romanze') included in his *Ritterballett* (WoO 1, 1790–1).
6 Although apparently not actually in residence there, Johann André was nominally the Kapellmeister of the Court Theatre at Schwedt.
7 In the accompanying letter he explained, 'You will find a lot of things crossed out in it; that's because I knew it was going to be copied here right away – so I gave my thoughts free rein – and before I handed it over to be copied, I made my alterations and excisions here and there. – Thus what you are getting is what was performed' (20 July 1782). It was a mark of distinction, Mozart observes in a later letter, that Riedesel had sought the score from him rather than purchasing it directly from the copyist (5 October 1782).
8 The playbill is reproduced in Hugo Fetting, *Die Geschichte der deutschen Staatsoper*, p. 65.

9 *Biographisches Lexikon des Kaiserthums Oesterreich*, Vol. 19 (Vienna, 1868), p. 284.

10 The sole modern scholar to challenge the authenticity of this document has been Wolfgang Sulzer, 'Bretzner gegen Mozart? Ein Protest und seine Folgen', *Acta Mozartiana* 29 (1982), 53–9.

11 6 (1783), p. 398. How telling the very orthography! Here Bretzner cites the title of his opera without a terminal *-e* on *Belmont*, exactly as it had appeared on the title page of the original libretto (Leipzig, 1781). Others, including the fabricator of the 1782 'protest', routinely use *Belmonte* instead of the form which Bretzner himself preferred in the title.

12 The revised version of the text has maintained its hold down to the present day in performances, recordings and editions of text and music. It can be compared with Stephanie's version in the edition of the libretto edited by Kurt Pahlen (Munich, 1980).

13 *Gedenkausgabe der Werke, Briefe und Gespräche*, Vol. 18, p. 894. I discuss Goethe's shifting attitudes toward German opera at this time more fully in *North German Opera in the Age of Goethe*, pp. 253–5.

14 *Dramaturgische Blätter*, p. 21.

15 *Singspiele von C. F. Bretzner* (Leipzig, 1796), p. iv.

16 In *Idomeneo* Weber finds 'all the colours familiar from Mozart's later works, displayed as it were on a palette'; here 'the weight of knowledge begins to struggle with the genius's delight in liberty'. *Die Entführung*, which celebrates 'the victory of youth in all its freshness', marks 'the first stage in that artistic condition which the world honours, marvels at and names after him "Mozartian perfection". . .It was only later that he achieved that exclusive conviction, the virile strength and presence of mind that were wholly dedicated to dramatic truth' (*Writings on Music*, trans. Martin Cooper, ed. John Warrack (Cambridge, 1981), pp. 264–5). No notice is taken in this organic model of the differing genres to which Mozart adapted his methods and aims in these operas.

17 *Allgemeine musikalische Zeitung* 28 (1826), pp. 835–6.

18 The Kärntnerthor Theatre had mounted a new production of the opera in 1801, but it enjoyed only a few performances.

19 *Die Entführung aus dem Serail* (Vienna: Wallishausser'sche k. u. k. Buchhandlung [Adolph W. Künast], n.d.). The main card catalogue of the Austrian National Library dates this edition at around 1900.

20 *Vertraute Briefe aus Wien*, Vol. 2, pp. 132–3 (letter of 5 April 1809).

21 *Allgemeine musikalische Zeitung* 46 (1844), p. 78.

22 Austrian National Library, Musiksammlung, T.W. 538 (prompter's book and two sets of parts – the shelf number indicates provenance from Schikaneder's Theater an der Wien) and S.m. 5056, 'Il Ratto dal Seraglio' (another prompter's copy); *L'Enlèvement du Serail*, arr. C. G. Neefe (Bonn: Simrock, [1799]); *Die Entführung aus dem Serail* (Hamburg: Böhme, 1823); *Il Ratto dal Seraglio*, arr. A. E. Müller (Leipzig: Breitkopf & Härtel, [1824]); *Die Entführung aus dem Serail* (Mannheim: K. F. Heckel, n.d.). Seidler, like some sopranos after her, may not have felt equal to the challenge posed by Constanze's two consecutive grand arias, Nos. 10 and 11, and so opted for the sorrowful, elegiac side

of the heroine's personality exploited by 'Traurigkeit ward mir zum Loose'. After this aria the Viennese libretto cited above in Note 19 carries a remark that, if it is sung, then the following scene is to be omitted together with its aria, 'Martern aller Arten' (p. 22).

23 *Allgemeine musikalische Zeitung* 14 (1801/2), pp. 320–2. Eventually Haselmayer decamped during the night without paying either his singers or the orchestra.

24 *A travers chants*, p. 243.

25 *Zeitung für Theater, Musik und Poesie* (Vienna, October–December 1807), pp. 38–9. The article, signed 'Adolph.', reviews a performance on 17 September 1807 by the Court Theatre.

26 *The Seraglio* (London: R. S. Kirby, 1828), pp. iv–v.

27 *Ibid.*, pp. 5–6. One wonders whether this scene might have reminded audiences in 1827 of the controversial deportation of the Elgin marbles two decades earlier.

28 Kramer's score, which survives in a published keyboard edition, is discussed by Alfred Einstein in 'The First Performance of Mozart's *Entführung* in London'. The text of Dimond's play was not available to Einstein, leading to some inaccurate conjectures in his article about the revised plot and the new characters.

29 *Allgemeine musikalische Zeitung* 42 (1840), pp. 921–2.

30 *Ibid.*, col. 925. Constanze Nissen and her husband in a letter to Carl mention a spinet, supposed to have been Wolfgang's, which they had lent to Lichtenthal (13 June 1810). He had befriended Mozart's widow and sons while studying medicine and music at Vienna from 1799 to 1809. In 1816 he published in Milan the first Italian biography of Mozart, *Cenni biografici intorno al celebre maestro Wolfgang Amadeo Mozart.*

31 *Opera* 7 (1956), p. 482.

32 Cynthia Solly in *ibid.* 8 (1957), p. 247.

33 The imperial loges were right next to the stage in the first rank of boxes, where Joseph could exercise strict supervision of a performance (see Plate 3).

34 Attila Csampi, *Die Entführung*, p. 202 (caption).

35 K. H. Ruppel, *Opernwelt* 9 (1965), p. 39.

36 Kurt Honolka, *Opera* 16 (1965): Festival Issue, p. 35.

37 Irving Kolodin, *The Metropolitan Opera*, p. 463.

38 *Glyndebourne*, pp. 95–6.

Bibliography

Abert, Hermann, *W. A. Mozart*, 9th ed., 2 vols and index (Leipzig, 1978 [revised and enlarged edition of Otto Jahn, *Mozart*])

Allgemeine musikalische Zeitung, ed. Friedrich Rochlitz, 50 vols (Leipzig, 1798–1848)

Allgemeiner Theater Allmanach von Jahr 1782 (Vienna, 1782)

Anderson, Emily, 'A Note on Mozart's Bassa Selim', *Music and Letters* 35 (1954), 120–4

Angermüller, Rudolph, '"Les Époux esclaves ou Bastien et Bastienne à Alger": Zur Stoffgeschichte der "Entführung aus dem Serail"', *Mozart-Jahrbuch 1978/79*, 70–88

Bauer, Wilhelm A., and Otto Erich Deutsch, *Mozart: Briefe und Aufzeichnungen, Gesamtausgabe*, 4 vols with 2 vols commentary and 1 vol index (Kassel, Basel, London and New York, 1962–75)

Bauman, Thomas, *North German Opera in the Age of Goethe* (Cambridge, 1985)

Beer, Adolf, ed., *Joseph II., Leopold II. und Kaunitz: Ihr Briefwechsel* (Vienna, 1873)

Berlioz, Hector, *A travers chants: Etudes musicales, adorations, boutades et critiques* (Paris, 1862)

Blumenthal, Lieselotte, *Mozarts englisches Mädchen*, Sitzungsberichte der Sächsischen Akademie der Wissenschaften zu Leipzig, Philologisch-historische Klasse, Vol. 120, Pt. 1 (Berlin, 1978)

Börne, Ludwig, 'Dramaturgische Blätter: Die Entführung aus dem Serail, Oper von Mozart [1818]', in *Sämtliche Schriften*, ed. Inge and Peter Rippmann (Düsseldorf, 1964), Vol. 1, p. 329

Bretzner, Christoph Friedrich, 'Vorrede', in *Singspiele* (Leipzig, 1796)

Chailley, Jacques, 'A propos de quatre mesures de l'Entführung: La renaissance de la modalité dans la musique française avant 1899', in *Bericht über den Internationalen Musikwissenschaftlichen Kongress Wien Mozartjahr 1956* (Graz and Cologne, 1958)

Croll, Gerhard, ed., *Die Entführung aus dem Serail*, Wolfgang Amadeus Mozart: Neue Ausgabe sämtlicher Werke [Neue Mozart-Ausgabe], Series 2, Work-group 5, Vol. 12 (Kassel, Basel and London, 1982)

Csampi, Attila, and Dietmar Holland, eds., *Wolfgang Amadeus Mozart: Die Entführung aus dem Serail* (Reinbek bei Hamburg, 1983)

Dabezies, André, 'Le Pardon dans les opéras de Mozart', in *L'Opéra au XVIIIe siècle: Actes du Colloque organisé à Aix-en-Provence par le*

Centre Aixois d'Études et de Recherches sur le XVIIIe siècle les 29, 30 avril et 1er mai 1977 (Marseille, 1982), 15–25

Daniel, Norman, *Islam and the West* (Edinburgh, 1960)

Dent, Edward J., *Mozart's Operas: A Critical Study*, 2nd ed. (London, Oxford and New York, 1947)

Deutsch, Otto Erich, ed., *Mozart: Die Dokumente seines Lebens*, Neue Mozart-Ausgabe Series 10: Supplement, Work-group 34 (Kassel, Basel, London and New York, 1961) [In English, with additions: *Mozart: A Documentary Biography*, trans. Eric Blom, Peter Branscombe and Jeremy Noble (Stanford, 1965)]

Dualt, Alain *et al.*, 'L'Enlèvement au Sérail', *L'Avant Scène*, 59 (January, 1984)

Einstein, Alfred, 'The First Performance of Mozart's *Entführung* in London', *Music Review* 7 (1946), 154–60

Mozart: His Character, His Work, trans. Arthur Mendel and Nathan Broder (New York, 1945)

Eisen, Cliff, 'Contributions to a New Mozart Documentary Biography', *Journal of the American Musicological Society* 39 (1986), 615–32

Fernandez, Dominique, 'La Figure du père dans les opéras de Mozart', in *L'Arbre jusqu'aux racines: Psychanalyse et création* (Paris, 1972), 189–291

Fetting, Hugo, *Die Geschichte der deutschen Staatsoper* (Berlin, 1955)

Floros, Constantin, 'Das "Programm" in Mozarts Meisterouvertüren', *Studien zur Musikwissenschaft* 26 (1964), 140–86 [reprinted with minor changes in his *Mozart-Studien I: Zu Mozarts Sinfonik, Opern- und Kirchenmusik* (Wiesbaden, 1979)]

Friebe, Freimut, 'Idealisierung und skeptischer Realismus bei Mozarts Frauengestalten', *Die Musikforschung* 26 (1973), 180–3

Friedel, Johann, *Briefe aus Wien*, 2 vols (Vienna, 1783–5)

Goerges, Horst, *Das Klangsymbol des Todes im dramatischen Werk Mozarts: Studien über ein klangsymbolisches Problem und seine musikalische Gestaltung durch Bach, Händel, Gluck und Mozart* (Munich, 1969)

Goethe, Johann Wolfgang von, *Gedenkausgabe der Werke, Briefe und Gespräche*, ed. Ernst Beutler, 24 vols (Zurich, 1949–54)

Gudewill, Kurt, 'Über einige "Töne" von volkstümlichen Liedern, Singspiel- und Opernliedern des ausgehenden 18. und des 20. Jahrhunderts', *Opernstudien: Anna Amalie Abert zum 65. Geburtstag* (Tutzing, 1975), 103–19

Haas, Robert, 'Einleitung', *Ignaz Umlauff: Die Bergknappen*, Denkmäler der Tonkunst in Österreich, vol. 36 (Vienna, 1911), ix–xxxiv

Hammer, Karl, *W. A. Mozart - eine theologische Deutung: Ein Beitrag zur theologischen Anthropologie*, Ph.D. dissertation, University of Basel (Zurich, 1964)

Heartz, Daniel, 'Mozart's Overture to *Titus* as Dramatic Argument', *Musical Quarterly* 64 (1978), 29–49

Hildesheimer, Wolfgang, *Mozart*, trans. Marion Faber (Frankfurt, 1977; New York, 1982)

Hochstöger, Susanne, 'Gottlieb Stephanie der Jüngere: Schauspieler,

Dramaturg und Dramatiker des Burgtheaters (1741–1800)', *Jahrbuch der Gesellschaft für Wiener Theaterforschung* 12 (1960), 3–82

Hocquard, Jean-Victor, *L'Enlèvement au Sérail (Die Entführung aus dem Serail) précédé de Zaïde* (Paris, 1980)

Hughes, Spike, *Glyndebourne: A History of the Festival Opera Founded in 1934 by Audrey and John Christie* (Newton Abbot, London and North Pomfret, 1965)

Jungk, Klaus, *Tonbildliches und Tonsymbolisches in Mozarts Opern*, Ph.D dissertation, Friedrich Wilhelm University (Berlin, 1938)

Keller, Hans, 'The *Entführung*'s "Vaudeville"', *Music Review* 17 (1956), 304–13

Killer, Hermann, *Die Tenorpartien in Mozarts Opern: Ein Beitrag zur Geschichte und Stil des Bühnengesangs* (Kassel, 1929)

[Knigge, Adolf Freiherr von], *Dramaturgische Blätter* (Hanover, 1788–9)

Kolodin, Irving, *The Metropolitan Opera, 1883–1966: A Candid History*, 4th ed. (New York, 1966)

Kunze, Stefan, *Mozarts Opern* (Stuttgart, 1984)

Laaff, Ernst, 'Prozess um Mozarts "Entführung"', in *Symbolae historiae musicae: Hellmut Federhofer zum 60. Geburtstag* (Mainz, 1971), 190–3

Lange, Joseph, *Biographie des Joseph Lange K. K. Hofschauspielers* (Vienna, 1808)

Liebner, János, *Mozart on the Stage* (London, 1972)

Litteratur- und Theater-Zeitung, ed. Christian August von Bertram, 7 vols (Berlin, 1778–84)

Mahling, Christoph-Hellmut, 'Die Gestalt des Osmin in Mozarts "Entführung": Vom Typus zur Individualität', *Archiv für Musikwissenschaft* 30 (1973), 96–108

Mann, William, *The Operas of Mozart* (London, 1977)

Meierott, Lenz, 'Der "flauto piccolo" in Mozarts "Entführung aus dem Serail"', *Acta Mozartiana* 12 (1965), 79–84

Meyer, Eve R., '*Turquerie* and Eighteenth-Century Music', *Eighteenth-Century Studies* 7 (1973/4), 474–88

Michtner, Otto, *Das alte Burgtheater als Opernbühne: Von der Einführung des Deutschen Singspiels (1778) bis zum Tod Kaiser Leopolds II. (1792)*, Theatergeschichte Österreichs, Vol. 3: Vienna, Pt. 1 (Vienna, 1970)

Nicolai, Friedrich, *Beschreibung einer Reise durch Deutschland und die Schweiz, im Jahre 1781. Nebst Bemerkungen über Gelehrsamkeit, Industrie, Religion und Sitten*, 12 vols (Berlin and Stettin, 1783–96)

Niemtschek, Franz, *Leben des K. K. Kapellmeisters Wolfgang Gottlieb Mozart, nach Originalquellen beschrieben* (Prague, 1798)

Nissen, Georg Nikolaus von, *Biographie W. A. Mozarts*, ed. Constanze von Nissen (Leipzig, 1828)

Osborne, Charles, *The Complete Operas of Mozart: A Critical Guide* (New York, 1978)

Pahlen, Kurt, ed., *Wolfgang Amadeus Mozart: Die Entführung aus dem Serail, Completter Text und Erläuterung zum vollen Verständnis des Werkes* (Munich, 1980)

Pezzl, Johann, *Skizze von Wien: Ein Kultur- und Sittenbild aus der josefinischen Zeit*, ed. Gustav Gugitz and Anton Schlossar (Vienna, 1786–90; Graz, 1923)

Preibisch, Walter, 'Quellenstudien zu Mozart's "Entführung aus dem Serail": Ein Beitrag zu der Geschichte der Türkenoper', *Sammelbände der Internationalen Musik-Gesellschaft* 10 (1908/9), 430–76 [an earlier version of pp. 430–57 was published under the same title as the author's Ph.D. dissertation (Friedrich Univ., Halle-Wittemberg), Halle, 1908.]

Questa, Cesare, *Il ratto dal Serraglio: Euripide, Plauto, Mozart, Rossini* (Bologna, 1979), 47–114

Rech, Géza, 'Bretzner contra Mozart', *Mozart-Jahrbuch* (1968/70), 186–205

Reichardt, Johann Friedrich, *Vertraute Briefe geschrieben auf einer Reise nach Wien und den Oesterreichischen Staaten zu Ende des Jahres 1808 und zu Anfang 1809*, ed. Gustav Gugitz, 2 vols (Munich, 1915)

Riekmann, Sonja Puntscher, *Mozart: Ein bürgerlicher Künstler: Studien zu den Libretti "Le Nozze di Figaro", "Don Giovanni" und "Così fan tutte"* (Vienna, Cologne and Graz, 1982)

Schenk, Erich, 'Zur Entstehungsgeschichte von Mozarts "Entführung aus dem Serail"', *Musik im Kriege* 1 (1943/4), 12–13

Schindler, Otto G., 'Das Publikum des Burgtheaters in der Josephinischen Aera: Versuch einer Strukturbestimmung', *Das Burgtheater und sein Publikum*, Vol. 1, Österreichische Akademie der Wissenschaften, Philosophisch-historische Klasse, Sitzungsberichte, vol. 305: Veröffentlichungen des Instituts für Publikumsforschung, no. 3 (Vienna, 1976), 11–95

Schink, Johann Friedrich, '*Die Entführung aus dem Serail*, komische Oper in drei Aufzügen, von Brezner, die Musik von Mozard', *Dramaturgische Fragmente*, Vol. 4 (Graz, 1782), 1001–25 [reprinted without acknowledgment in *Magazin der Musik*, ed. Carl Friedrich Cramer, 2:2 (1784), 1056–79]

Schubart, Christian Friedrich Daniel, *Ideen zu einer Aesthetik der Tonkunst*, ed. Ludwig Schubart (Vienna, 1806 [written 1784–5])

Schweizer, Hans Jörg, 'Bassa Selim', in *Sodalitas Florhofiana: Festgabe für Professor Heinz Haffter zum fünfundsechzigsten Geburtstag am 1. Juni 1970* (Zurich, 1970), 140–9

Szabolcsi, Bence, 'Exoticisms in Mozart', *Music and Letters* 37 (1956), 323–32

'Mozart et la comédie populaire', *Studia musicologica* 1 (1961), 65–91

Tenschert, Roland, 'Pedrillos Romanze', *Allgemeine Musikzeitung* 68 (1941), 303 [reprinted as 'Die Romanze des Pedrillo: Bemerkungen zu einer seltsamen Komposition von Mozart', *Österreichische Musikzeitschrift* 3 (1948), 301–3]

Teuber, Oscar, *Geschichte des Prager Theaters. Von den Anfängen des Schauspielwesens bis auf die neueste Zeit*, 3 vols (Prague, 1883)

Theater-Zeitung für Deutschland, ed. Christian August von Bertram (Berlin, 1789)

Ujfalussy, J., 'Intonation, Charakterbildung und Typengestaltung in Mozarts Werken', *Studia Musicologica* 1 (1961), 93–145

Ungarese, F., 'Die Entführung aus dem Serail. Ein deutsches Singspiel in drey Akten', *Zeitung für Theater, Musik und Poesie* 3 (1808), 361–5

Weber, Carl Maria von, *Writings on Music*, trans. Martin Cooper, ed. John Warrack (Cambridge, 1981)

Werner, Richard Maria, ed., *Aus dem Josephinischen Wien: Geblers und Nicolais Briefwechsel während der Jahre 1771–1786* (Berlin, 1888)

Gallerie von Teutschen Schauspielern und Schauspielerinnen nebst Johann Friedrich Schinks Zusätzen und Berichtigungen. Schriften der Gesellschaft für Theatergeschichte, Vol. 13 (Berlin, 1910)

Whaples, Miriam Karpilow, 'Exoticism in Dramatic Music, 1600–1800', unpublished Ph.D. dissertation (Indiana University, 1958)

Wilson, W. Daniel, *Humanität und Kreuzzugsideologie um 1780: Die 'Türkenoper' im 18. Jahrhundert und das Rettungsmotiv in Wielands 'Oberon', Lessings 'Nathan' und Goethes 'Iphigenie'* (New York, Bern, Frankfurt and Nancy, 1984)

'Turks on the Eighteenth-Century Operatic Stage and European Political, Military, and Cultural History', *Eighteenth-Century Life*, 2:9 (1985), 79–92

Würtz, Roland, 'Das Türkische im Singspiel des 18. Jahrhunderts', in *Das deutsche Singspiel im 18. Jahrhundert: Colloquium der Arbeitstelle 18. Jahrhundert Gesamthochschule Wuppertal Universität Münster* (Heidelberg, 1981), 125–37

Wurzbach, Constant von, *Biographisches Lexikon des Kaiserthums Oesterreich*, Vol. 19, 'Mozart, Wolfgang Amadeus' (Vienna, 1868), 170–295; Vol. 38, 'Stephanie, Gottlieb' (Vienna, 1879), 222–5

Wyzewa, Théodore de, and Georges de Saint-Foix, *W.-A. Mozart: Sa vie musicale et son oeuvre de l'enfance à la pleine maturité (1777–1784)*, Vol. 3: *Le Grand Voyage, l'installation à Vienne* (Paris, 1936)

Discography

S	Selim	Versions:	A	Overture, 1–4, 5b–21b
C	Constanze		B	Overture, 1–4, 5b–14, 16, 15, 18–21b
Bl	Blonde			
Be	Belmonte		C	Overture, 1–4, 5b–10, 12–14, 16, 15, 18–19, 11, 20–21b
P	Pedrillo			
O	Osmin		(m)	monophonic recording
			(4)	cassette version
			(e)	electronically reprocessed stereo
			(c)	compact disc

all recordings are in stereo unless otherwise indicated

1936 Korner *S*; Piltti *C*; Beilke *Bl*; Erb *Be*; Zimmermann *P*; Strienz *O*/Reichssender Chorus and Orch., Berlin/Heinrich Steiner
Version unknown — ANNA (m) 1019

1945 Schwarzkopf *C*; Loose *Bl*; Dermota *Be*; Klein *P*; Alsen *O*/Vienna Radio Chorus, Austrian Radio Orch./Rudolf Moralt
Version A (6 omitted) — Melodram (m) MEL 047 (private)
Broadcast performance with dialogue omitted; issued in 1982.

1947 Hargrave *S*; Steber *C*; Alarie *Bl*; Kullman *Be*; Garris *P*; Ernster *O*/Metropolitan Opera Chorus and Orch., New York/Emil Cooper
Version unknown — EJS

1950 Woester *S*; Lipp *C*; Loose *Bl*; Ludwig *Be*; Klein *P*; Koreh *O*/Vienna State Opera Chorus, Vienna Philharmonic Orch./Josef Krips
Version B — Decca (m) LXT 2020/21
Decca Eclipse (m) ECM 730/31
London (m) LLP 227/9 (LLPA 3)
Richmond (m) RS 63015
Originally issued on 78 rpm.

1950 Gyurkovics *C*; Gencsy *Bl*; Rösler *Be*; Kishegyi *P*; Székely *O*/Hungarian State Opera Chorus and Orch./Otto Klemperer
Version B — Hungarotron (m) LPX 12636/37

1954 Frank *S*; Stader *C*; Streich *Bl*; Häfliger *Be*; Vantin *P*; Greindl *O*/RIAS Chamber Chorus, RIAS Symphony Orch., Berlin/Ferenc Fricsay
Version B — DGG (m) DGM 18184/5
DGG (m) 2700 010
DGG (e) 2730 014 (reissue)
DGG-Heliodor (m) 89756/57
Decca (m) DL 9785/6 (DX-133)

Live performance of 20 March 1950 (Hungarian State Opera); sung in Hungarian with dialogue omitted.

1954 Tyler *C*; Petrich *Bl*; van Kesteren *Be*; Schiebener *P*; Griebel *O*/Cologne Opera House Chorus, Gürzenich Orch. of Cologne/Otto Ackermann
Version B (17 omitted) — Discophilia ⓜ KS 20/21
Musical Masterpiece Society ⓜ M 113
Concert Hall Records
A concert version with dialogue omitted.

1956 Laubenthal *S*; Marshall *C*; Hollweg *Bl*; Simoneau *Be*; Unger *P*; Frick *O*/Beecham Choral Society, Royal Philharmonic Orch./Sir Thomas Beecham
Version C — EMI (Columbia Electrola) ⓜ IC 153–01541/42 (SLS 5153)
reissue: 157–01541/42 (mono)
HQS 1050/1 (stereo)
Angel ⓜ 35433/4 (SB 3555)

1961 Wolf *S*; Pütz *C*; Holm *Bl*; Wunderlich *Be*; Wohlfahrt *P*; Littasy *O*/Vienna State Opera Chorus, Mozarteum Orch./István Kertész
Version unknown — Melodram ⓜ 702/3 (private)
Live performance of August 1961 (Salzburg Festspiel).

1962 Schütte *S*; Vulpius *C*; Rönisch *Bl*; Apreck *Be*; Förster *P*; van Mill *O*/Dresden State Opera Chorus, Dresden Staatskapelle/Otmar Suitner
Version A — Philips ⓜ A 02230/31 L
835118/19 AY (6720 005)
Philips-Fontana 700 194/5 WGY
Turnabout TV 34320/21

1964 Spiess *S*; Walbrunn *C*; Benda *Bl*; Börner *Be*; Köthner *P*; Jürgens *O*/Patagonia Festival Chorus and Orch./Ralph de Cross
Version A (13 & 17 omitted) — Period ⓜ TE 1102
Live performance with cuts in many numbers.

1965 Boysen *S*; Köth *C*; Schädle *Bl*; Wunderlich *Be*; Lanz *P*; Böhme *O*/Bavarian State Opera Chorus and Orch., Munich/Eugen Jochum
Version A — DGG SLPM 139213/5 (mono: LPM 39213/5)
DG Privilege 2726051
DGG Mozart-Edition ④ XIV
Phonogram 6747 387
The set also includes Mozart's *Bastien und Bastienne*, K.50.

1966 Rudolf *S*; Rothenberger *C*; Popp *Bl*; Gedda *Be*; Unger *P*; Frick *O*/Vienna State Opera Chorus, Vienna Philharmonic Orch./Josef Krips
Version B — EMI-Electrola 1 ⓒ 197–00070/71
World Record Club SOC 235/6
Seraphim SIB-6025

1968 Kelsey *S*; Dobbs *C*; Eddy *Bl*; Gedda *Be*; Fryatt *P*; Mangin *O*/Ambrosian Singers, Bath Festival Orch./Yehudi Menuhin

Version A — EMI (HMV Angel) SAN 201/3
EMI SLS 932

Sung in English; dialogue by Hugh Mills, musical texts by Joan Cross and Anne Wood.

1973 Mellies *S*; Auger *C*; Grist *Bl*; Schreier *Be*; Neukirch *P*; Moll *O*/Leipzig Radio Chorus, Dresden Staatskapelle/Karl Böhm

Version A — DGG 2563 284/6 (2709 051)
(4) 3371 013

Includes Mozart's *Der Schauspieldirektor*, K.486.

1979 Leipnitz *S*; Gruberová *C*; Ebel *Bl*; Araiza *Be*; Orth *P*; Bracht *O*/Bavarian Radio Chorus, Munich Radio Orch./Heinz Wallberg

Version A — Ariola-Eurodisc 300 027–440
(4) 500 027–441

Studio broadcast of October 1979.

1979 Jürgens *S*; Eda-Pierre *C*; Burrowes *Bl*; Burrows *Be*; Tear *P*; Lloyd *O*/John Alldis Choir, Academy of St. Martin-in-the-Fields/Colin Davis

Version A — Philips 6769 026 4 7699 111

1985 Reichmann *S*; Kenny *C*; Watson *Bl*; Schreier *Be*; Gamlich *P*; Salminen *O*/Chorus and Mozart-Orch. of the Zurich Opera House/Nikolaus Harnoncourt

Version A — Teldec 6 35673 (digital)
(4) 4 35673
(c) 8 35673

On film:

1967 Pasetti *S*; Rothenberger *C*; Blegen *Bl*; Krenn *Be*; Stolze *P*; Czerwenka *O*/RIAS Chamber Chorus, RIAS Radio Symphony Orch., Berlin/Georg Solti

Version A (with 12 & 13 reversed, 17 omitted)
Sets: Jean-Pierre Ponelle *et al.*/Direction: Heinz Liesendahl/Photography: Werner Kunz/110 minutes, colour. The dialogue is shortened and completely rewritten.

1980 Holtzmann *S*; Gruberová *C*; Grist *Bl*; Araiza *Be*; Orth *P*; Talvela *O*/Bavarian State Opera Chorus, Bavarian State Orch., Munich/Karl Böhm

Version B
Sets: Max Bignese/Direction: August Everding/120 minutes, colour. Live performance (Munich National Theatre).

1980 Bissmeier *S*; Masterson *C*; Watson *Bl*; Davies *Be*; Hoback *P*; White *O*/Glyndebourne Festival Chorus, Orch./Gustav Kuhn

Version A
Sets: William Dudley/Direction: Peter Wood/129 minutes, colour.

Index

Note: tables and bibliographic citations are not included.